THE TWO MAGIC CODE WORDS TO WEALTH

SCRIPT AND FLAME

A TREASURE SCROLL OF GOLDEN SUCCESS SECRETS TO FOLLOW IN LIFE, AND HELP YOU BECOME A MILLIONAIRE

B.K. Haynes

Copyright © 2017 B.K. Haynes

All rights reserved.

Greatland Publishing

ISBN: 978-0932586049

wwwscriptandflame.com

I went upon the mountain top
And prayed for earthly gain
The secret rules revealed to me
Are found in **Script and Flame**

B.K. HAYNES

AT AGE 80 I BEGAN TO COMPOSE
MY PERSONAL 20-YEAR PLAN AND
GUIDEBOOK FROM HERE TO ETERNITY

ACKNOWLEDGEMENTS

The sure sign of knowledge comes quickly down to us in the written page. Knowledge, of course, if focused properly and not diffused, can also lead to power and the ability to achieve your goals in life. It is my feeling that knowledge, in the general sense of the word, exists only to be shared. With this thought in mind, I decided to write down what I learned in life and to pass it on. In December 2016, while recovering from shoulder implant surgery I completed this work.

The following people helped me pull this book together: my associate, poet and writer, Louise Clark; my assistant, Eileen Zehring; creative consultant, Jeanne Russell; my pastor and spiritual counselor, Jay Ahlemann; and Charlie Thorne of Charles Thorne Graphics.

CONTENTS

CHAPTER	Page #
Foreword	vii
Preface	xiii
1 Racing through Life	1
2 SCRIPT and FLAME	9
3 Develop the Savings Habit	15
4 Learn the Art of Accurate Thinking	21
5 Have Confidence in Yourself	37
6 Master the Art of Self Control	45
7 Master the Power of Concentration	73
8 Act to Cooperate with Others	79
9 Practice the Golden Rule	89
10 Use Your Imagination	95
11 Develop a Pleasant Personality	103
12 Practice Tolerance and Patience	115
13 Learn to Profit from Failure	123
14 Learn to Lead and Harmonize with Others	137
15 Have a Definite Chief Aim in Life	147

CHAPTER	PAGE #
16 Go the Extra Mile	163
17 Act With Enthusiasm	169
18 Adopt the Spirit of Courage as You Age	177
A Treasure Scroll of 16 Success Rules	196
19 Action Points	197
Appendix 1 – Summary of Lessons Learned	203
Appendix 2 – Cash Flow & Net Worth Sheets	205
Appendix 3 – 16 Rules (3a-3l)	207
Back of the Book	239
Item 1 – Ageless Thoughts from the Guard of Wisdom	240
Item 2 – The Chilling Power of the Human Mind	244
Item 3 – The Love Boat to Heaven	256
Item 4 – 16 Ways to Use the Bible in Your Path Thru Life	259
Item 5 – Laughter – It's Good for You	264
Index	268
Bibliography	276
About the Author	279

FOREWARD

In 2015 I asked a colleague for a reference to a Realtor in the Front Royal, Virginia countryside. Without hesitation Keith recommended I contact B.K. Haynes. He then explained that B.K. was no ordinary realtor, which peaked my curiosity because Keith knew I had moved countless times in my career and had likely met every kind of Realtor. And so began my relationship with B.K. When I first met him shortly after that referral it was clear that B.K. was far from ordinary; in fact, was truly extraordinary. After several days spent with him exploring the countryside it was clear to me that B. K. was a true "renaissance man" in every sense of the word. Our time, while searching for the property of our dreams, was also an academic treat for me. I was afforded the incredible opportunity to hear the humble tales of a man who had a career as a self-made entrepreneur, to ask of him unlimited questions, and to learn from his readily shared experiences. B.K. possesses a generosity of heart and a desire to share his wisdom, nearly all of it from practical experience, and does so in this work. It's not every day one comes across a successful business man, former soldier, singer, song-writer, screen play-writer, realtor, developer, rancher, horse trainer, teacher and even less frequently when that someone is gentle and humble and kind.

SCRIPT AND FLAME

I recall B.K. first telling me about a new book he was writing, and when I asked him about its subject the answer took me a bit by surprise. Our conversation turned elsewhere, and it was some time before the subject of the book resurfaced, and that was through my inquiry. He advised me it was nearing completion and asked me if I'd care to read it myself. I readily agreed, as I was already intrigued with this persona and any chance to gain further insight into what makes him tick was certainly welcome. I was subsequently honored when asked to consider writing this foreword. I was also shocked to learn B.K.'s age as a result of this review, as he presents himself as a man of far fewer years, which after reading this book, I better understand (and likewise hopefully learned part of) "the secret."

As a recent retiree, who Lord willing, still has a lot of life to live, and wants to do so to the fullest, this book was a Godsend to me as it holds many life lessons and provides insightful wisdom as to the keys to success in our remaining years, no matter how many they may be. A key point is that *"it ain't over til it's over"* and there is much to be accomplished, much life to be lived, many graces and experiences to be shared, and that our final years can be every bit as good, or even better, than the earlier years. As a father, government executive, and perhaps with the most impact as a leader of troops in combat environments, I have always subscribed to two mantras, "Run to the finish" and "Make luck happen," and have encouraged all under my care to do the same. Doing so is a best path for success, maintaining personal integrity, staying safe, and ensuring you do your best in all things at all times. While the words are different, these very mantras are clearly exhibited in this book, and B.K.'s anecdotes and stories ring them loud and clear for the reader.

In his charmingly good natured way, B.K. lays out numerous opportunities for the reader to ensure they too have the necessary keys and hence are enabled to prosper well into the "good old age." There are many "secrets" to success in life, and while financial success is but one measurement, B.K. is quick to identify there is much more to successful living than the bottom line of one's net worth. As B.K. likes to do, and frequently does so well as he spins his yarns of wisdom with dramatic or influential quotes and references, I end this foreword citing the title of a movie starring my favorite actor of yesteryear, the late, great Jimmy Stewart, in *You Can't Take It With You*. Jimmy Stewart never met B.K., or at least that I am aware of, but there is no doubt in my mind that the great actor lived up to the standards of a life well lived, and lived well, that B.K. Haynes provides the very prescription for living in this wonderful literary work.

Ken Reuwer

SCRIPT AND FLAME

About the writer of the foreword:

Ken Reuwer is a true subscriber to the life lessons exhibited in this book. Hard work, determination, passion, personal and professional integrity, and always seeking to do what's right are paramount traits in successful living.

Ken spent two years in a Capuchin Seminary in Herman, PA in the 1970s where he had incredible mentors, teachers and truly formed his life-long game plan. While the priesthood was not to be, he married a close friend from his high school years, and after 33 years they have six children in ages from 24 to six, each of which, along with his wife Michelle, is one-seventh part of his greatest legacy.

After a brief stint in the US Army Corps of Cadets as an ROTC scholarship student at Johns Hopkins University in his hometown of Baltimore, MD, Ken finished his Bachelor's degree at Virginia Tech. His approximate 30-year federal career started as a Special Agent with the Defense Investigative Service in Annapolis, MD and in Bangor, ME. After a transfer to the Central Intelligence Agency, Ken had the opportunity to travel to and work in over 70 countries. He later joined the ranks of the Special Agents of the Naval Investigative Service, later becoming the "NCIS" and completed tours of duty in Camp Lejeune, NC, London, UK, Naples, IT, Norfolk, VA and the greater Washington, DC area. His most memorable assignments were as a legislative fellow for the Department of the Navy, with a Congressional Office in the 109th Congress, solving a "cold case" from 1966 in Scotland, serving two tours of duty as the Operations Chief for the Strategic Counterintelligence Directorate (SCID) in Baghdad, being a first responder to the bombing of the U.S.S. Cole, and ultimately working in over 100 countries during his career, and making life-long friendships with persons the world over. "Special Agent Reuwer" rose to the rank of Deputy Assistant Director, and his last tour of duty was as the Chief of the Joint Counterterrorism Coordination Cell (JC3), in Quantico, VA. In his "retirement" Ken works as a counter-intelligence advisor for another government agency, is the Commissioner of a 7-team youth baseball league, which he created several years ago (and coaches his youngest children's teams), is on the board of his homeowner's association, and is an active member of the National Rifle Association, as well as the Rappahannock Valley Civil War Roundtable in Fredericksburg, VA. Ken has many other hobbies as time allows, along with his children, including rifle and pistol shooting, golfing (poorly; but pleasurably), fishing, hiking, U.S history, site-seeing, and current events.

PREFACE

Prospering at Any Age

Everyone is a student of someone else - B.K. Haynes

At 80 years of age, life can appear to be a day at most. This book is written by a working author and rags-to-riches businessman who is racing the sundown of life about two decades past the time clock of retirement for most readers. Possibly a third or more of your gift of life from God may yet to be opened to you. Yesteryear's age 62 is the new 72. In 2016, a survey of active seniors at my church revealed an average old age of 70, a figure that could have been closer to a ripened figure of 60 in the 50's; and, at 82, I was the oldest one at the party. If you are in the Springtime of aging you must prepare for the Fall. Technology now siphons away the outdated jobs of disengaged mid-lifers, many of whom cannot find satisfaction in this brighter and better world. Social Security replaces only 40% of the average American's income; and savings are generally insufficient to help maintain a comfortable retirement. Poor health and family care-giving issues tend to aggravate the situation.

Experts on aging point to increased life expectancy as evidential proof of a future clash of generations, thrusting elders into a defensive parameter within society as a whole. But the emerging army of younger citizenry may be less mighty than they seem, because many have inherited (1) a general weakness in spirit because of declining religious beliefs; (2) questionable projections about their future; (3) the spoiling of tradition, with the adoption of tainted political and social narratives; (4) the erosion of honesty in societal thought and action; and (5) the lack of full compassion for agers, the bulk of whom are now sailing into the heart of darkness as the imminent force of undying youth takes control of the populace and exhibits more than a gentle annoyance for the presence of their doddering seniors and their unbalanced and existential need for government handouts.

In my youth, never in my wildest dreams did I embrace the notion that money makes possible the best the earth affords. I simply envisioned all the good things and various career fields that I thought would bring me happiness and contentment. I grew up on the streets of our nation's capital, where our family's lack of money—not our will—consented to the steady din of street car tracks. The only childhood family gathering that I can recall is a newspaper photo of me, three other straight-faced siblings, and a dog, Silver, posing as empathetic media feed for the felonious jailing of my father, a "wise guy" outlier and failed writer, with the pen name, Bradley K. Haynes. My mother was once a poor and pubescent farm girl, who grew up with few soothing memories—a child maid for a wealthy family; and later a strip model; an unfulfilled writer; a college dropout—but a dutiful mother married to a life of poverty.

Chapter 1
RACING THROUGH LIFE

At age 8, I was caught sneaking into the theater and grilled on where my father was. My innocence was shaken when I replied, with tears, "He's in jail." I was struck where I was most vulnerable—the need for a boy to respect his father as a man. **At age 10**, I was peddling newspapers, diving for tourist pennies in the fountains of Union Station, and hauling boxes of "relief" food for the poor, dumped on the curb in front of our row houses. Heroic figures in my young mind in those days were movie cowboys; warriors fighting against Japan and Germany; saintly soldiers of the Salvation Army; social workers who care for the sick and poor; and preachers who open the doors and windows of the gospel to the downtrodden and to those of meager means faced with hunger, danger, sickness, and despair. All of these noble figures, it seemed, gave more than they received. Richness of heart, in my mind, trumped the topic of wealth. Little did I know in my youth that all ways of life are open to those with money—down to the masses living on paved roads aimed at goodness and prosperity to those poor souls trudging along pot-holed streets toward crime and a life of poverty. **At age 12,** my 8-child family was moved by welfare officials into a public housing unit in the emerging suburbs of D.C. where, for a precious quarter or two, I hauled baskets of truck-dumped coal in my little red "Radio" wagon from the curb to the coal bins of paycheck-to-paycheck residents in a shanty, white-only development, where we had few friends, no church, no community ties. We could scarcely have been more foreign than in a ghetto of the passive rotting mass.

At 13 and 14, I earned money by nursing a paper route and carrying condiments to the men in the screening booth at the local movie house, where I was granted free movies—this pleasant task performed after football or baseball games and practice. I learned to play the harmonica and wanted to move up to the guitar; but I had to settle for a ukulele, when my dad snatched the fifteen dollars set aside for lessons to pay for family food.

At age 15—after my family had broken up and three of the siblings had been sent to a charitable church home—I quit the vocational high school, where I studied commercial art and was holed up for a winter of discontent in cheap hotel rooms and on cold city streets with a traveling band of lost souls led by con artists hawking questionable magazine subscriptions from door to door in low-rent neighborhoods without character or form. This was my job after having been recruited by a glib shyster to travel through the exciting and enchanting environment of the Rio Grande. Being trustworthy and unfamiliar with the laws of money, I left my hard-earned cash "on the books" and in the hands of the shysters, who vanished in the night after I requested a withdrawal of my meager funds.

Fumbling in my early manhood, I later got a job as a messenger boy and picked up a measure of vocabulary by reading word cards while I hoofed it through the streets of Washington D.C., past edifices of a world apart, like the White House and the Capitol building. This was a step up to reading books. My errant father once asked me if I read books and I told him, "no." Learning to be a full man had yet to come.

Racing through my teens, I worked at various low-paying jobs, living in rooming houses and attending night school, while singing pop songs on the radio and emceeing variety shows for the D.C. Department of Recreation at local military facilities such as Quantico in Virginia and Walter Reed in D.C. Towering in confidence, I was hell bent on becoming a famous crooner like Frank Sinatra; but two years in the Army—as a graduate and instructor from Leadership School, and an ambulance driver in Fort Myer (the quarters for high level generals, and situated outside of Washington D.C. and the nation's Home of the Unknown Soldier)—I found compassion in both doctors and generals; and I quickly learned that that I didn't know much about life and that I needed to broaden my education. While in the Army, I obtained a GED certificate, stating that I had met high school graduation standards. *In my 20's*, I had worked my way through George Washington University on the GI Bill, earned a BA degree in Business Administration, traded romance for marriage, chipped away at a master's degree in communication, wrote songs, played the guitar, and sang folk ballads for free at local clubs. I remained a singer before I grasped the outward effects of fame, riches and female companions; and I continued to hear this calling before I knew that the trackless past of my less-than-tropic youth was gone.

Reflecting on my lack of money while living on my wife's paycheck as a bookkeeper, I opted to take a job with General Electric, advertising their appliances. "Hoist your dryer sales!," I wrote. I dutifully wore a gray-flannelled suit, carried a lunch box, and punched a time clock, earning about $600 a month. I hated foul language but was forced to use it to act tough against competitors in the business world. After seven months of servitude to a corporation that could have given me wealth in exchange for my soul, I quit, becoming an apostle of personal freedom, fighting my transformation into an Organization Man, while escaping to a cabin in the woods with my wife and guitar and vowing to never work for anyone other than myself for the rest of my life.

I then set-up a nickel-and-dime vending machine business, with offices in my sparse apartment; and at *age 27*, I moved up in life, buying five acres with a shell cabin and starting a riding stable in nearby Virginia where my ancestry had plunged from nobility in England to the ranks of a Hessian soldier in the Revolutionary War.

It never occurred to me that I was on the threshold of wealth; and little did I know at the time was the fact that the safe use of wealth without reason offers about the same degree of relative assurance to a man as a horse without a bridle. But we will learn more about the perils of unexpected wealth as we proceed with this story.

In 1964, the real estate market was exploding, as the recreational land boom took hold across the nation. The pockets of the middle class were jingling with discretionary coinage, and more and more people could afford to own land in the mountains, the valleys, along lakes, rivers, and the sea. It soon became clear to me that the history of the 20th century was on a fast track to be determined by the cities and not the countryside, for an oak tree never sleeps while its acorns slip away.

All of us are educated by defeat, and it is the stimulus of defeat that gives us encouragement to reach out for a better life. I had a small home, a stable of nags, a few bucks in my pocket, and an ominous shadow of creeping debt about to engulf me and wipe out my meager holdings. In the early 60's, hard-working people like cab drivers, dishwashers, laborers, and even the underprivileged and socially-emerging blacks, were plunking down $50 dollars and paying $50 dollars a month to own a small lot in the nearby countryside. This eventful socio-economic movement in the D.C. area amounted to an invasion into the realm of the bourgeois by the lower class—a force that began breaking convention and the devilish chains of poverty.

Good news about the economy and increased wages stirred the life-blood of the blue collar and vassal classes, following a plague of grief over the assassination of the popular savior, President John F. Kennedy, whose Camelot estate in Middleburg, Virginia remained an establishment imprimatur of the moneyed and social elite. Vulturine thoughts like, "Without my dole, I'm done," began to flee from the minds of the lower class. The years of elitist long knives seemed to wane in the face of cultural change.

Across the river and railroad track divide, separating the city "come heres," from the cultured elite, there were people of wealth who owned mansions surrounded by rock fences and fields grazed by thoroughbred horses. The rich were philanthropic in their charities, and generous with their families. They were bountiful with their expenses. And it seemed to me—a young and penniless saddle bum—that their wealth appeared to increase more rapidly than they spent it. My idealistic mind however, never drifted to thoughts that rich people should descend from their thrones so that everybody would have the same. I learned later in life that I was reduced to little more than bare existence, because I had failed to embrace the mysterious rules that govern the accumulation of wealth.

Gone with the wind were the perils of my riches: millions of dollars, my airplanes, my home in Hawaii, my farm, my camp, paintings, gold, silver, thousands of acres fallen from my asset base like snow, then blown away into drifts for banks and creditors. I penned a lyric from this perilous instrument of life: **"I had money once; I had money twice; but when I lost it all, My friends were not so nice."** The dying world of the years 2007-2016 was without faith, hope, character, or full understanding of its malady or will to overcome it. Then, like Lazarus, I returned from the dead and, once again, broke the chains of idealistic thought.

Regardless of what you are or what you have been, you can still be what you want to be.
– W. Clement Stone

Nine years of mental wandering saps the mind's investment in an adult's life. Whether you are at the mid-life of your career, or if your career has left you behind, the wise man is one who realizes that he cannot know everything. As for experience, remember this: Experience is often overrated by the old and entrenched, who are embattled by successive disenchantment with the entangled web of life. There is no correlation between higher education or tenure in one's calling and the accumulation of wealth, love, or power. Only the great principles of life endure and—to nurse the soul—these points you must commit to memory and use them to build habits.

In general terms, a man is thirty years old before he has any settled thoughts of his fortune; it is usually not completed before fifty, and he stumbles and often falls while *a-building* toward the years when his thoughts eventually give way to the grand question of life, "Will I go to Heaven?" By cultivating the rules about to be revealed to you, your habits will become quite different from the ways of those who are swamped in a morass of failure and despair when they draw near their eternal home; and by recognizing this difference, you take the first step toward prospering in twice your childhood, when the physical, mental, social, and spiritual aspects of your life will be challenged to degrees you may never have imagined. Use this book as your *Manifesto of Travel* through the cloudy skies of your journey through life—a God-given passport from this world to the next—for the days of your life are waning, their strength, labor, and sorrow may soon be cut off; and you will fly away.

> *I have learned to be content with whatever the circumstances. I know what it is to be in need, and I know what it is to have plenty. I have learned the secret of being content in any and every situation, whether well fed or hungry, whether living in plenty or in want* – Philippians 4: 11-12

Prayer of Serenity

God grant me the Serenity to accept the things I cannot change, Courage to change the things I can and the wisdom to know the difference.

Chapter 2
SCRIPT and FLAME

Shakespeare said that it is mind power that makes the body rich. And, like the body, the mind can be disjointed. Evil empires, such as Hitler's 3rd Reich, have been created and crushed by the thoughts of mankind. The study and function of imaginative thought patterns—used for good or evil—can be characterized as a form of scientific endeavor. Thoughts, in effect, are natural forces like words and fire.

If you read the *Bible* you will find numerous accounts of spiritual visions, clairvoyance, and telepathy. When fate wills that something should come to pass, she sends forth a million little circumstances to clear and prepare the way. Napoleon declared that he controlled circumstances—that he refused to be the victim of happenstance. (He also asserted that women, by the nature of their thought processes, made their own circumstances—this without particular reference to circumstantial control.) Therein lays a great secret known only to the most successful achievers on earth, though many tycoons and tyrants may act on this secret primarily through their subconscious mind. Many intelligent and discerning people fervently believe that the conscious control of circumstances is crucial to determining your future and your fate in life. But you should understand that this admonition applies primarily to life's challenges, lest we forget that we are all purpose-driven children of a righteous and holy God when shaping our character.

Of course, if you lose control over your mind, either through disease, torture, hypnosis, or brain washing, this citadel of your senses could fall and your thoughts would be unguarded—your path in life then measured by your soul. If you comprehensively read or listen to the contents of this book and master the given rules—all with *Biblical* verification, rather than just a sage's ancient historic vision of mankind evolving from the womb—you can prosper at any working age. Below are the secret code words to unlock the chains of thought that may be holding you back from reaching your goals in life.

NATURAL FORCES = WORDS and FIRE = *SCRIPT* and *FLAME*

In college of my day, the word, SCRIPT, often meant the form in which you were to answer a written examination. It is also derived from the word, SCRIPTURE, which is a sacred book or writing, commonly known in the Christian world as the *Bible*. The code word, **SCRIPT**, then, could mean answers written down that you should live by. **SCRIPT** is a powerful word—a principal code word in this case—formed from key letters of ten proven principles behind the achievement of a more pleasing life and success at any working age.

SCRIPT AND FLAME

Without words, man could not govern the world, create pictures of our thoughts, or express the voice of our heart. Without words, man could not have become man—nor women, woman. The 2nd principal code word you should commit to memory—and subsequent action—is the word, **FLAME**. Fire is the most tangible of all visible mysteries. It is evidential combustion; a bright light to lead the way; voracious, all-consuming energy; the sun, the sustenance of life on earth. It made man independent of climate, gave him a greater compass on earth, tempered his tools to hardness and durability, and gave him as food a thousand things inedible before.

Hidden in the word, **FLAME**, are the six remaining primary principles for success at any productive age—most uncovered by Napoleon Hill—as being endemic in the lives of successful men that he researched, analyzed, and interviewed during his time on earth. The word, **FLAME**, can be your guiding light to the earthly treasures and happiness at the far end of life's tunnel.

The word, **SCRIPT**, can only serve as your map and guide to the tunnel's entrance; and you can only proceed as far as daylight can penetrate. Together, these two amazing words—**SCRIPT** and **FLAME**—can unlock a storehouse of treasures and contentment such as your mind has never seen. In a well-measured life, I am not solely talking about the accumulation of riches. Wealth is shy and timid; it won't come to you. It is totally the antithesis of poverty, a condition which, in a bold and ruthless way, can overtake wealth, whenever it accumulates without well-conceived and carefully executed plans. To observe this truth, you have merely to recall the *Biblical* parable of the profligate son and to observe the flight of wealth around the world from the twin evils of inflation and communism.

In Og Mandino's inspiring book, **The Greatest Salesman in the World**, the author tells of the rich merchant's remark to the aspiring young camel boy who would become a wealthy and successful salesman. "So far as material wealth is concerned, there is only one difference between myself and the lowliest beggar inside Herrod's palace. The beggar thinks only of his next meal; and I think of the meal that will be my last."

With these leveling thoughts in mind, and with the knowledge that whatever thoughts you send out will come back to you greatly multiplied to bless or curse, let us proceed to unravel the secrets of success at any stage of your life—**16 rules in all**—that I found hidden within the words, **SCRIPT** and **FLAME**. Remember that these rules are not just expedient thoughts for this hour of your life alone; they are laws for the young, and for persons past their second childhood.

The truly successful people in the world have acquired a state of mind in which they are convinced of their success, no matter at what age they achieved satisfaction in life. Remember, those who fail are those without the ability or initiative to reach their goals, whatever they may be. And failure has never been known to overtake the person whose will to succeed is strong enough. At three score and ten—even four score years or more—we may not be ready to be cut off to fly away, because the glory of an April day may still lie ahead in our thoughts and aspirations.

Now consider the fickle friend of life's decline—blessed retirement. The happy person who retires at 60 may be making a sad mistake; for when he or she quits work, they risk becoming deficient in their mental and physical activities and abilities, thus taking on a faster pace to the grave. Like the young car parked for decades in an old barn, humans rust and die when they remain unused. For a century, mankind believed that old age began at 50; now it is an age to prepare for eternity

This thought had long been imbedded in the subconscious mind; now the noiseless feet of aging time are racing on past 80, and the human body still remains active. **Pursuits soon become habits, and habit and imitation are the source of all working, all apprenticeship, all practice, and all learning in the world.** Your objective should be to restore and form good habits and to become their slave. As for the perception of agedness, the state of your declining years can be left to the eye of the beholder; or better yet, the mind of the beheld. In the *1970's* I was in my *early 40's* and worth a million. I envisioned owning a ranch, and soon found it after traveling to Africa, where the vision (*desire*) took form (*belief*). I returned with stirred emotions (*enthusiasm*) and quickly found my dream ranch (*accomplishment*).

Chapter 3
(S)CRIPT AND FLAME RULE # 1
Develop the SAVINGS Habit

Babylonian parables teach those of us who are security driven and financially ambitious to set aside a portion of our hard-earned money, no matter how small the amount. We are taught through lectures, observation, books, and the fiery litany of financial wizards, that all riches in the world have limits, and that when all is spent or lost from our earnings, it may be too late to reap liberty from the dreaded prison of poverty. Frugality, it is taught, is a fair fortune for the future. It is written that we must look at the aged, and not forget the days to come, because we also will be numbered.

Here hangs a twice-told tale that happened in 1923, so long, long ago, preceding the Great Depression of 1929. This story-telling reveals the fact that successful careers of the wealthy cover a multitude of blunders and can often cost more than they are worth. The tale can be found in a library of books on fortune building. Who knows if any of these storied men were born in a cellar? Certainly, all of them trotted up the stairs to a bountiful life. Eight of the world's greatest financiers, anchored in wealth, once met in Chicago. The group included (1) the president of the largest independent steel company; (2) the president of the largest gas company; (3) the greatest wheat speculator; (4) the president of the New York Stock Exchange; (5) a member of the President's cabinet; (6) the greatest bear on Wall Street; (7) the head of the world's greatest monopoly; and (8) the president of the Bank of International Settlement. And then what happened?

Sixty years later, it was learned that they had all fallen into the hellish abyss of squandered time and wealth. The president of the largest independent steel company, Charles Schwab, died a pauper. In the last few years of his life, he was plagued to live on borrowed money. The president of the world's largest gas company, Howard Hobson, lost his mind and died insane. The greatest wheat speculator, Arthur Colton, died abroad in tattered clothes. The president of the New York Stock Exchange, Richard Whitney, sank into the grave of crime, serving time in Sing Sing prison. The member of the President's cabinet, Alfred Fall, stumbled into crime and was later pardoned and released from prison so he could die at home. The greatest bear on Wall Street, Jesse Livermore, plucked death from the Maker's hand and died a suicide. The head of the world's greatest monopoly, Ivor Kruger, the Match King, found a remedy for a luxurious life in the pit of suicide. The president of the Bank of International Settlement sneaked away to death at the barrel of his own pistol pressed into his temple.

Despite the fact that much of my spare money in my stable days was invested in horseshoes, happiness was found through my own eyes and not through a prism reflecting another man's wealth and plan of life. I wasn't miserable being thrown by a horse. It came with the territory. Sure I had faced severe injuries, maybe death, engaging in hapless episodes like being dragged up a gravel road by a rogue runaway horse, when my foot was trapped in a lead line. Still, I never doubted that I would make a living as a small-change hack, running a horse-riding stable.

In 1964, during my early days as a neophyte in real estate, I will never forget dining on burgers in a beer joint with husband-and-wife friends—whose lives were better served than mine—when, in front of my wife, I was confronted with a comment from my male friend that a future in real estate was dark for a stable hack. This was a low point in my life. I realized then that life is a walking shadow, a tangled rope of good and bad moments following our tracks. Looking for ways to expand my stable operation, I had invested—along with two acquaintances from my rural community—in a farm joining the vast Shenandoah National Park, where I would enjoy almost unlimited territory to ride horses, and where we would develop a subdivision of recreational building lots that we could flip to city dudes for $50 down and $50 a month. The selling farmer evidently assumed we were rich; though we had to hustle down-payment money from several small loan companies. Consequently, we were able to wrap up a simple owner-financed deal. **The assumption of wealth is often as good as being rich.**

In August of 1965, at age 31, I was saddling up for a trail ride in the Blue Ridge mountains when a dude told me the National Guard had been called to attention by a bloody carnival in Los Angeles—an imploding cradle of crime called Watts. The city was in flames. That same day, what I had been fell from me like dirty rags. I burned the bridges behind me and hit the trail for my adventures in country properties. The salesman on duty at our development joining the Shenandoah National Park was suddenly unavailable. Paying customers were breaking down the doors in response to my first ad. And I was called out to sell land. I had never aspired to be a land salesman and often referred prospective land buyers to the sales people in my development, while requesting no compensation.

Many land projects across the country—a few funded by nationally known corporations—had turned blind eyes to a corrupt land development system staffed with aggressive sales people. These robotic hustlers often viewed customers as "pigeons" —dupes caught in a sweat cage and doomed for plucking by platoons of fast-talking dirt peddlers. The high-pressure ordeal then led to their release to a secondary sales force, where the saps were further clipped of any hesitancy-to-buy objections by militant "closers" who would routinely verbally beat up any creep who merely hinted at refusing to buy a lot in Paradise. This sales process may sound weird in an internet world of casual bargain searchers; but that was how lots and land were hustled by a roster of big developers pushing dirt in the 60's and 70's.

In 1959, *at age 25*, after graduating from George Washington University, I had written radio and television commercials for an ad agency; so I had a feel for brevity in advertising. My first thought on ad writing was to avoid positioning property for sale as part of a residential development. I lived among the maddening crowd and recognized the inherent limitations on freedom of movement within communities; so I began advertising individual parcels of affordable land.

I prodded my horse, Buddy, into a trailer and rode off to the development where, in over a few weeks, I sold out the land from horseback. Along the way, I'll always remember a customer in one of my early projects referring to me as a developer; although I will confess—a financially poor one at best. **But to be poor, and to seem poor, is a certain method for strivers to never to rise up in life.** I decided that *at age 31*, that I was behind the curve on the road to success, and that the surest way to avoid a crash in my journey toward a better life was to determine to succeed; so some rough and uncertain days of study would lie ahead

MONEY LESSON LEARNED: Save 10% of what you earn, but not at the cost of liberality. Have the soul of a king and the hand of a wise *Economist*.

Chapter 4
SCRIPT and FL(A)ME RULE #2
Learn the art of <u>ACCURATE</u> Thinking

To retain the pleasure of your youth, you must first be at peace with yourself, and this means, essentially, knowing your own mind, taking control of it, and directing it accurately toward a specific goal(s). Obviously you are searching for elusive happiness, economic success, and security, or you would not be reading this book; and you are certainly aware of the frustrations, worry, and deprivation that befall those without sufficient money in their possession. It should be obvious, too, that aside from monetary success, you also will want to be free from fear, tension, self-induced illness, and ignorance. These negative forces are your enemies, and they find refuge and succor in minds plagued with similar negative attitudes. A mind dominated by accurate thoughts makes the body rich and guides you toward your goal of mental health and stability, forming a barrier against intellectual decay. Within the realm of reality, it is crucial for the open mind to discard or avoid adopting any habit of delusion. Such a habit, often cultivated in certain political circles and radical secular crusades, can open the doors to hysteria and violence whenever the root of delusion is touched. **It is said that if you do not follow your own thoughts, then you will follow the thoughts of others**; so let's examine those principal inaccurate thought patterns that stalk weak minds, hoping to totter thoughts toward negativism and failure. An enemy discovered is an enemy half-whipped.

INACCURATE THOUGHT PATTERNS

1. Needless worry and feelings of inferiority or being left out

2. Feelings that you can't surmount poverty and want

3. "Neuroticism" brought on by suspicions and unwanted fear

4. Allowing fear to bring about feelings of failure

5. Seeking something for nothing

6. Allowing others to control your mind

7. Dissatisfaction with (and griping about) one's work or situation

8. Doing no more than what you are paid for, or obligated for

9. Mourning over petty misfortunes

10. Expecting rewards and benefits prior to giving them out

11. Cultivating the negative emotions toward life and your fellow man

12. Encouraging indolence in charitable work

13. Making excuses for unfulfilled objectives

These *thought patterns* are your enemies, and you should bolster your defenses against them by clearing away the cobwebs in your mind. It is not wise to take the faults of our youth into our length of days—for aging brings its own faults. Clear and accurate thinking depends, **First**, on separating the facts from information and opinion. **Second**, you must separate the chaff from the wheat by disposing of that which is unimportant or irrelevant. **Third,** you must learn to think with your mind and not your emotions. We often find ourselves the dupes or victims of our own extremities. You are interested in achieving certain goals in life without sacrificing your peace of mind; for it is clear that a mind at war with itself cannot lead you to fulfillment in life. Our brains continue to change throughout our lifetime, shaped by our thoughts, experiences, and intentions.

To gain control of your mind, you must first root out any enemies lurking there. Your objective is to secure more accurate thought patterns and to know your own mind. A preacher and legitimate man of God would tell you to follow the thought patterns of Jesus; and you would know that he is not trying to fill your mind with falsehoods.

On the other hand, a political hack or false friend may forcefully tell you that you know not what you do by voting for the con-man candidate or the candidate of yesteryear—that, in fact, you have lost control of your mind.

Begin to re-enforce your thought patterns by pinning down the following **enemies and working to destroy their build-up in your mind**:

ANGER	HATRED	SLANDER
CRUELTY	HYPOCHRONDRIA	UNDEPENDABILITY
DECEIT	IMPATIENCE	OBSESSIVE VANITY
DISHONESTY	INDECISION	WORRY
DISLOYALTY	INJUSTICE	EGOTISM
INSINCEREITY	ENVY	INTOLERANCE
FALSEHOOD	JEALOUSLY	FEAR
LUST	GOSSIP	MERCILENESS
GREED	REVENGE	

The easiest thing for us to discover in a failing life, and the hardest thing for us to discover in ourselves, is that we are becoming more foolish and wiser, and that we are running out of money. We are now aware of laws that protect us later in life from job discrimination. **Put your talents into practice and distinguish yourself, and don't think of retiring from work until the world will be sorry that you retire.**

It is fatal to be forced into a corner by pride, cowardice, or laziness and to do nothing but sit and growl, when you can step forth and bark. Women, in this respect, are blessed, for they can do one job while thinking of many other things. For both men and women, we have employment assigned to us for every circumstance in life. When we are alone, we have our thoughts to watch; in the family, our tempers; and in company, our tongues. We worry about health and wealth, seeking inward peace; and money issues ring in our ears all the time. So make all you can, save all you can, and give all you can.

There are four basic ways for people to increase their income:

1. **Scratch each other's back in business.**
2. **Showing the other person how he can get more for his money.**
3. **Bringing the producer and the consumer closer together.**
4. **Saving a portion of all you earn and sharing opportunity with those of similar intent, inclination, and drive.**

Life will frequently crumple for us, even in hearts beating under three-score winters, if we do not have some hobby, talent, or other subsidiary activity that will act as support for any occupational commitments and other income sources. It is not an easy task to be constantly aware of the infiltrating negative thoughts that can wear down your health, wealth, independence, and peace of mind; but considering the stakes, it is worth the effort. Late in life, the cards are not dealt in your favor for reforming your thoughts and habits, since time is the king of men. In the words of Shakespeare, ". . .time is their grave, and gives them what he will, not what they crave." The Bard also said, "Time is the nursery and breeder of all good." Therein lies our hope for change and improvements in our thoughts, attitudes, and actions. The mind can be easily kidnapped through intensive brainwashing by educational institutions, false religions, corruptive governments, and media bias.

Here is a list of 50 questions you should ask yourself to determine the current accuracy of your thought patterns. (*Free speech recess is given here for emotional outbursts and expressions emanating from political and sports activities and protests against perceived unjust laws, regulations, and legal rulings.*)

1. **Do you too often erupt with unmerited anger at people, or in other ways lose unnecessary control of your emotions?**
2. **Do you slander and condemn people?**
3. **Do you seek revenge for any real or imagined injustices done to you?**
4. **Do you often lose your poise under unfavorable circumstances?**
5. **Do you ever think that other people "owe" you a living, and that you "can't" accomplish what you want to do?**
6. **Do you find yourself constantly bragging and boasting to raise your self-esteem?**

7. **Do you often feel as if you have to do something immediately, without giving it sufficient thought?**

8. **Are you always griping and complaining about people and things?**

9. **Do you express contempt for new ideas, proposals, and changes prior to examination?**

10. **Do you often feel that your life is hopelessly in the hands of someone else?**

11. **Do you harbor and openly express any racial and non-violent religious prejudices?**

12. **Is your mind filled with unjustified fear about anything or anyone?**

13. **Do you think of yourself as an expert on all subjects?**

14. **Do you readily speak about the faults of others?**

15. **Are you slow to forgive, forget, and restore positive thoughts?**

16. **Are you always in a state of tension, worry, and anxiety?**

17. **Are you easily led by ideologies foreign to you and your country?**

18. **Are you constantly at war with your family and mankind?**

19. **Do you make enemies easily?**

20. **Do you begrudge having to share your blessings?**

21. Do you draw back from expressing gratitude to God or man?

22. Do you express opinions without being in possession of the facts?

23. Do you allow your mind to drift, steering toward indefinite goals?

24. Are you unable to cope with excess in eating, drinking, and other unhealthy habits?

25. Do you wink at transactions which are profitable to you and harmful to someone else?

26. Do you bemoan defeat as anything but a temporary setback?

27. Do you often see other people as uncooperative?

28. Do you "play dirty" with adversaries?

29. Do you doubt the existence of a power greater than yourself—a power that is available to you if you seek it diligently?

30. Do you become morbid and unglued after disappointments?

31. Are you always apologizing for not doing your best?

32. Are you quick to accuse and blame others?

33. Do you keep the door to the past open in your mind?

34. **Do you discount the existence of certain eternal truths about mankind in relationship to his environment?**
35. **Do you allow negative thoughts to dominate your mind?**
36. **Do you rationalize about getting into debt and take repayment lightly?**
37. **Do you make liabilities of adversities and defeats, rather than turning them into assets?**
38. **Are you unduly disturbed by panics and depression in the economy?**
39. **Do you often wish you were someone else?**
40. **Do you sense that certain classes of people dislike you?**
41. **Do you ever find yourself trying to live someone else's life for them?**
42. **Do you allow your mind to run away with thoughts of wealth?**
43. **Do you aspire to have more money than you can comfortably use?**
44. **Do you talk about your success to others, rather than letting your accomplishments speak for themselves?**
45. **Do you look for the seed of an equivalent benefit in all of your failures?**

46. **Are you guilty of lazy thinking about a main goal and how to obtain it?**
47. **Are you too quick to trust and too slow to verify?**
48. **Do you rage beyond mind control at un-solicited marketing calls?**
49. **Can you hold back anger when younger peers treat you as a child?**
50. **Do you blow up when family members try to make decisions for you?**

A classic example of inaccurate thinking follows: In 1968, money was pouring in from my land projects in three states and from my brokerage operation. One day at a project on the Chesapeake Bay, I was introduced to a slick character who claimed to have been the financial manager for Rocky Graziano, the famous prize fighter. The guy was pitching a grand scheme to promote a Shopper's Passport credit card entitling consumers to receive cash rebates for purchases from selected merchants. This "pass" was the precursor of the Discover Card. Sensing a need to diversify my business operations, I cleansed myself of excess cash and became a player, with control of international franchise rights. I remember the brains of the operation—a computer that filled an entire room and that performed tasks now accomplished by a laptop.

At the time, my brother-in-law was working for a bank on the West Coast, helping to kick off the new MasterCard. I hastily imported him and his family to the D.C. area, mantled him with a vice presidency, and charged him with authority to help build this house of cards. Within a year, he was back on the West Coast, fed up with the whole escapade. I should have seen the bats among the birds when the Passport promoter said he needed a few grand to fly down to St. Vincent for a pow-wow with some moneyed CEOs. I said I would like to go down for the ride. For reasons I can't remember, he said he didn't think it was a good idea. The whole scheme eventually collapsed into a fraud investigation, and I had to fight a bloody audit when I claimed legitimate losses to lessen the heavy tax gains on my first million.

Thoughts are free, yet they rule the world; so you'll want to keep them accurate. If you can truly answer "no" to all of the above questions you could rightfully be called a genius in knowing what you want out of life and how to reach your goals and obtain your objectives without losing your peace of mind. <u>Someone once said that genius is the ability to see the pattern of things and to project those patterns</u>. **The key to accurate thought patterns lies in your ability to identify and eventually destroy those enemies of the mind mentioned earlier. When you have done this, you will find yourself in possession of amazing powers unknown to most of mankind.** Of course, the person who has no enemies has no following; and a man who makes no enemies is never a positive force.

Regardless of your political opinions, consider, for example, the career of Donald Trump. The glory and pitfalls of his legend endures. Over the years, his

reputation was sold at a cheap market by his political adversaries. Yet the falsehoods were not always so. Trump's riches were the results of his wisdom as a leader and his uncanny acumen as a businessman. He first had to learn how to become wealthy. His route to success is to (1) Think big; (2) Stay focused; 3) Keep your guard up; (4) Be passionate; (5) Never give up; and (6) Love your work. I have researched and studied the man and read every pre-election book written about his controversial life, this with the objective of academically measuring his political viewpoints and capabilities as a leader.

When Trump moved his construction operation into Manhattan, the heart of New York City, after a round of successful projects in the boroughs, the young upstart was rewarded with nothing more ridiculous than ridicule itself. After his early business years of building modest homes, apartments, and projects for the poor, he ventured forth into his real love—the impetuous scheme of building skyscrapers, cities within cities, world-class hotels, casinos, and time-honored golf courses spread over several continents.

Beyond the perils of wealth, Trump's construction achievements in the private sector rivaled the public authority accomplishments of Robert Moses, the idealistic New York master planner who, aside from alleged graft and the normal practice of patronage, reached out into the thinly populated suburbs, building parks, bridges, highways, and housing projects that essentially transformed an already decaying city into the blemished realm of a bustling New York City as we know it today.

At age 69, Donald Trump was one of the richest men in the world, fiercely tackling the political establishment of the Republican party in a bold run for the presidency, while hiring hundreds of thousands of people along the way. Another measure of statistics in 2016 was that he was poised to wear the mantle of a sitting president racing close to age 80. And in terms of personal conception, no other president in the history of the United States came anywhere near Trump—as an individual—in building so much private sector infrastructure and accumulating wealth on such a dynamic scale. Of course, history will determine his destiny.

But there was a time for the young Trump when hundreds of thousands of workers were without employment. Merchants were faced down with fewer customers. Retailers were no longer looking for outlets to sell their products. Office and store space became the home of bats and mice. The people had less money to buy food and clothing. Trump's casinos in Atlantic City were financially aflame, threatening an even fiercer hell to his empire. And where had all the money gone that was spent for all of these empty buildings?

The villains were reported to be the big banks and robber barons aligned with Wall Street wolf men, through whose fingers the people's money was filtered faster than milk through a strainer. The populace, it seemed, was left with nothing to show for their siphoned earnings.

Donald Trump was thoughtful for a time; then he asked himself about the besmirched and deteriorating skyline of Manhattan—spiraling structures of concrete and steel, vaster than the pyramids - that once consumed a million men. "Why should so few men be chosen to build these monstrous architectural edifices, many of which remained half empty in New York City?" Of course, the answer was blowing in the wind. These favored builders had power through the influence of politically entrenched officials in the court of local government, an empire within an empire that governs every inch of ground and air space in the city. Who can condemn a man who succeeds because he knows how?

The Donald Trump saga is interesting because it shows a pattern of behavior identifiable in great leaders on both sides of the political aisle who have accumulated great wealth and power. All great leaders do not necessarily exhibit all of the true qualities of statesmanship; nor do they need to follow all of the prescribed rules of success. Obviously, Trump's coffers to finance his run for the presidency were full enough to cure any dependency on the donor class. Trump's ultimate legacy could very well be his outreach to others on how to acquire and keep riches by the utilization of many age-old principles, even if this knowledge comes to you late in life. When asked what thoughts he would have if he had lost the presidency, he indolently replied, "I think it would be a terrible waste of time and money." He took pride in stride, hiding his own inevitable hurts and moving on not to hurt others.

With reference to Trump's theatrics, Shakespeare said, "Assume a virtue if you have it not." He also said, "Something is rotten in Denmark." Trump was able to change his political demeanor from bullish to sheepish at the swipe of his childish hand. The contest exposed an alleged rottenness of the political voting system in the 2016 presidential election. We are already aware of the need to develop a savings habit. Money begets money. We also know that our thoughts are free and that we must practice them accurately, lest we be reduced to servitude and choked by our imperfections.

MONEY LESSON LEARNED: Accurately assess your expenditures. Don't let your desires eat up your savings.

Chapter 5
S(C)RIPT and FLAME RULE #3
Have CONFIDENCE in yourself

You've probably noticed that, as we age, our entire emotional state changes. We lose flexibility in our bodies, slowing down our mindset. New ideas and ways of thinking tend to lose momentum. Older folks may seem more set in their reactions and opinions than their younger counterparts. Physical therapists know that exercising, and moving around, makes people more agile on their feet and quicker in their thought processes. People hunching over and drooping their heads when they walk are generally characterized as old folks. Their body movements tend to drain the power of human physiology, lowering confidence levels and leaving the impression of a person with low energy.

All of us could use a little more self-confidence in our lives. As we observe others of greater or imagined success, we tend to focus on this characteristic of self-assurance. When prominent personalities appear before us, we often feel as if we are viewing individuals of sublime self-confidence. Self-conceit (ego) exists to a large degree in prominent personalities; though we may not perceive this symptom at all. What we see in successful people is an intense identification of that person with his object of interest or work. Common fears, such as danger and death, can seem beneath the concern of that personality. The person's past achievements, or immediate efforts, could appear almost unattainable to the common eye; and we are awed by what we perceive to be an almost superhuman will of accomplishment.

Think for a moment of Lindberg preparing to cross the Atlantic alone; Joe DiMaggio extending a record hitting streak of 56 consecutive games that appears safe for 500 years; Gary Cooper, alone at *High Noon*. Self-confidence is the first requisite to great undertakings. Only when many of your hopes have failed, and when your fears have passed unrealized, can you expect to build self-confidence. You are the judge of how your own internal forces relate to the outside world. It would seem, then, that you must first **ADMIT** your strengths and weaknesses—all of your hopes and fears.

Consider the worst of human conditions—The Abysmal Failure. He is incapable of earning much money. He is continuously quarrelsome. Nobody does anything he suggests. In sports, he is clumsy and slow. All of the hobbies he ever tried were flops. He can't get along with his own family. He's lousy at work and **ADMITS** he shouldn't get paid for what he does. He can't talk anybody into anything. He laughs at what he cannot learn. Everything goes wrong for him. If it were not for bad luck, he'd have no luck at all. He gets conned into sucker schemes. Kids shake him down for money. He's convinced that everyone is looking down on him.

Now, since it is unlikely that anyone reading this book considers him or herself an abysmal failure, we can surmise that there is hope for anyone to raise their level of self-confidence. **Fear and doubt, of course, are the real reasons why people lose confidence in themselves and are specifically the rationale for courting distrust in others.** The absence of fear—and not higher education or high I.Q.—is the major factor of individual success in life.

Thoughts of doubt and fear always lead to failure.

It would seem that our Abysmal Failure was beyond hope because of his cancerous fears. Only a miracle could possibly save him. But miracles, being children of faith, have been known to occur; and fear is the primary reason why the Creator, or Infinite Intelligence, does not always affirmatively respond to prayer. Belief in a higher being than yourself (faith) is an absolute first step in the building or rebuilding of self-confidence. We may have blundered through youth, struggled with manhood, and now, for many of us, we may feel we have reached an age of regret. Yet even the ageless, and the worst failures and reprobates in our society, can find their minds and lives reshaped by a newly-found and abiding faith. It is the lynchpin in the development wheel of character and self-assurance.

In the process of cultivating self-confidence, your mind will be given certain exercises to perform. The role of faith in this process is to enlighten and guide the mind. Every person is a creation of themselves.

The first exercise I want your mind to perform is quite simple. You must **ADMIT** to yourself that there is a higher being (God, if you will) or Infinite Intelligence, greater than any man or woman on earth, and that you have the same opportunity as anyone else of communicating and forming an alliance with this miraculous source of all energy and life itself.

Every successful man or woman has received help from unknown sources—whether or not the assistance or talent is acknowledged as a spiritual gift; so don't think for a minute that self-confidence comes solely from developing your own internal forces.

Napoleon Hill writes about the form of self-hypnosis called *Autosuggestion*—a mind exercise in which the subconscious mind is influenced to act automatically on your wishes or desires. It is a powerful force for personal achievement, especially when coupled with prayer (your means of connecting with God, or Infinite Intelligence). Through effective prayer, you express a fervent and persistent plea for help in the attainment of certain hopes, desires, and definite objectives, which you ADMIT

you cannot attain through efforts of your own. Original accomplishments, such as inventions, musical scores, novels, plays, and poetry, and technical and medical discoveries, are all given birth (visualized) in the subconscious mind. The primary functions of the conscious mind are: reason, logic, basic form, judgment, calculation, and moral sense. This multi-form of belief, of course, would enter your life through your conscious mind when your body is in danger. Your deeply held beliefs originate in your subconscious mind.

Now you may have noticed the number of times I used this word, **ADMIT**, in this brief discourse; and you've seen that I have capitalized it like the previous code words, **SCRIPT** and **FLAME**. The word **ADMIT** is comprised of key letters in my formula for raising your level of self-confidence. When working to develop this essential principle of success, you can remember the points on which to concentrate by referring back to the word, **ADMIT**.

A-D-M-I-T = YOUR SELF-CONFIDENCE FORMULA

A = Autosuggestion – Your doorway to the subconscious mind, where, through the process of self-hypnosis, your desires, hopes, and definite chief aims, if held persistently, will express themselves in some practical way. The subconscious mind, through its link to Infinite Intelligence, will bring forth rewards, benefits, and fulfillment in direct proportion to those things that one thinks about most often and to those objectives and desires that one believes are attainable. Some religions, spiritualists, dictators, political extremists, and tyrants misuse this subliminal and repetitious form of mind control to catechize their dictums and spread messages that often evolve from published ego-driven manifestos.

D = Definite Goals – All individual achievement begins with definite purpose and a written or mental plan for its accomplishment. The subconscious mind will not act upon ideas, opaque plans, or purposes.

M = Mental Attitude – A contagious state of mind which communicates itself from one person to another without spoken words, signs, or actions, by the medium of telepathy; therefore the attitude should be positive. Thoughts mixed with feelings of emotion tend to attract similar or related thoughts. The elements of success or failure in our lives are usually shaped by attitudes, rather than mental capacity.

I = Can! – The firm belief that whatever the human mind can conceive and believe, the mind can achieve. Knowing (1) exactly what you want, and (2) going after this goal with enthusiasm and total commitment, will alert you to opportunity. You are what you want to be, including when you have the smack of age and some relish of the saltiness of time. You act as you want to act. Here's how a wise poet has expressed this thought.

If you think you're beaten, you are;
If you think you dare not, you don't.
If you like to win, but you think you can't,
it's almost certain you won't.

If you think you'll lose, you've lost;
for out of the world we find.
Success begins with a person's will—
it's all in the state of mind.

If you think you're outclassed,
you are; you've got to think high to rise.
You've got to be sure of yourself,
before you can ever win a prize.

Life's battles don't always go
to the stronger or faster one.
But soon or late the one who wins
is the person
WHO THINKS THEY CAN!
- Walter Wintle

T = Truth and Justice – Your realization that nothing can be received without giving something of equal value in return and that every adversity, every unpleasantness, every failure, and every physical pain carries, with it, the seed of an equivalent benefit. In a spiritual sense, the benefit comes from a higher and most righteous power—God if you will, with whom you must establish, or reinstitute, an eternal friendship through (1) humble thought; (2) devoted discipleship; (3) sharing with others; and (4) frequent prayer.

Whatever you do for another by the thoughts you set forth, so shall you reap. Love always rebounds to those who express it, even though it may not be reciprocated.

If you want people to speak well of you, then never speak well of yourself; though politicians may cry down the egos of their enemies while masking their own faces and demeanor.

Better to present yourself before a full-length mirror. Great orators like Winston Churchill and Adolf Hitler used this technique to lift the confidence levels of their people and to make the orator appear more formidable. Evangelists and actors have followed suit with rehearsal stints before mirrors. The method boosts subconscious forces flowing from their speech and dialogue. Salesmen have perfected the "mirror method" to trick the minds of others into buying items and services from a dominant force.

MONEY LESSON LEARNED: Great fortunes are not built in a day, but come as dollars adding themselves to those saved.

Chapter 6
S(C)RIPT and FLAME RULE #4
Master the art of Self CONTROL

Now on to a fourth proven success rule for those fleeing the faults of youth, it is necessary to sharpen up our minds, particularly in the declining years of our money-making lives, when opportunities for building financial security are facing exile in our thought processes, and where, for some inheritors of old age, the concept of retirement has been relegated to the elder's humble existence in a vacant shack, barn, or garage, with even scarce enough money to buy this book.

Shakespeare said that crabbed age and youth cannot live together. It is understandable, in a society that worships success, that few people know how to be old. Aside from the necessity to control our emotions, particularly as we outdistance our youth, we are compelled to examine the ageless postulate of frugality, a concern that has been taught and promulgated by financial sages throughout the centuries. These wise men preach a mantra that states, **"He that is extravagant will quickly become poor,** and poverty will enforce unwanted dependence and invite corruption." A pitfall for the free and easy rich person would be a compulsion to pick up all checks at restaurants; or to be the host at every gathering.

Emotion, of course, is always new. And an outburst, turning back on itself, and not leading to thought and action, is the element of madness. As we humans transfigure or begin to petrify in the sunset of life, it is important to realize that feelings, like flowers, last longer the later they are delayed. The heart that is soonest awake to the flowers is always the first to be touched by the thorns.

Extreme sensitiveness, or quick unleashing of the tongue, can be harbingers of disharmony and displeasure in life. Of course, thoughts have wings and can be hurtful, fanciful, and impromptu—forming opinions and breeding illicit sexual desire, criminal activity, human abuse, and often soaring down on controversial issues and on other people with whom you disagree. Such thoughts pass through our minds like a noiseless train. To live better, you would best let the worst thoughts pass on, rather than allow them to become a station in your mind.

Whatever ventures that lie beyond the limits of experience, and claim another origin (such as a compulsion for idealism or creativity) that deviate from established talents and practice, can often leaden failed endeavors with painful consequences—both emotional and financial.

We look at many people harboring self-made riches, and we think how lucky they are; but we do not see the sacrifices they have made, the efforts that made them rich, the knowledge they possess, and the faith they have put forth to gain wealth and acclamation in their determined battle—not to become poor—but to overcome and defeat adversity.

Once upon a time, I had amassed a fortune and was unmasked by my accountant as a profligate spender, who wasted hundreds of thousands of dollars on material things and such misguided and unfamiliar projects as a camp—the quest driven by an all-absorbing goal from my idealistic days; a money-pit airport that sopped the coinage of my brain; a fleet of private cars; a bankrupt Branson, Missouri music show that emerged from my life-long aspiration for a musical career; and prodigious efforts to write and promote two screenplays that have long been gathering dust on producers' shelves in New York. All were a sleeping king's dreams, waking up to matter.

As time went by, I was asked a question that was repeated over and over by a legion of loan officers. "What exactly is your cash flow, Mr. Haynes? I simply explained that I was a real estate broker, primarily in the business of developing land. I said that business was slow and that my cash flow had dried up, the excuse made worse with the exposure of my profligate ways—because the gods of wealth will surely avoid an entrepreneur whose wallet is thin.

Years ago, when I operated a large land development corporation, the regional managers would bring deals to me and reason that—because the salesmen had little left to sell—the corporation should locate a project for them. On one occasion, we purchased some mountain land, primarily because it was cheap. And much of it was too steep for development. We entered the deal primarily because the land was cheap, and because our salesmen and the regional manager needed to be kept productive. Here is clearly a case of the tail wagging the dog. As you may suspect, the project was a loser, and we were forced to dump the property at close to the acquisition price when cash flow problems crept up on us.

One fellow I knew had a grand and glorious dream about creating an environmentally-sound and aesthetically-pure recreational community. Environmentalists loved the concept; architects were ecstatic over plans to blend their great creations with the great outdoors. Real estate organizations praised the venture as the wave of the future; salesmen took up the call and swore their ship would soon be coming in. The developer sailed blindly ahead, confident that his course was legal, just, and rightly served. Suddenly he was becalmed by planning agencies and government officials who felt threatened by higher density and a proposed rising tax rate in the county. With his sales flattened, the developer soon ran out of cash. His ship of fortune was beseeched with leaks—too many for him to plug. His supporters, sensing impending doom, jumped ship. Suppliers came upon the listless vessel and demanded payment. Lawyers moved in for the kill. In a desperate gamble, the developer grabbed onto the bankruptcy laws and reached relative safety—though he had lost his fortune.

My point is—and if you remember this well, **no matter where you are in the tangled web of life—to avoid losing those hard-earned dollars: YOU MUST PAY YOURSELF FIRST.** You can play with deals, donate to charities, assist others in business—and this spirit of helpfulness can make you feel good; but if others persuade you to override good judgment, you risk disappointment and failure. Life is as serious as death, with quicksand and snares ahead and behind us as we trod from job to job, build careers, and face the challenges of imagined obstacles. By conversing with what is above, the wise will take note of a dying flame and live by an invisible sun within themselves.

I cannot characterize my questionable decisions and actions as inaccurate thinking, because many of the elements have evolved from the instinct of talent and the essence of life itself. From what I will, I will. Practicing what I preach, I once fixed my mind on a second airplane, a Piper Super Cub, to fly from my private airstrip. During a separate deal, the seller said he also had an airplane I could buy with the assignment to him of notes receivable.

Of course, I knew then that my subconscious had delivered the Cub. In the twilight of age however, the aspect of **self-control** addresses the seven basic fears that shadow our financial issues and have varied degrees of influence on our thought processes. And thoughts, whirling like a potter's wheel, wander through eternity. I will discuss these seven fears momentarily.

There once was an orator in ancient Greece who said: "I'm sure he could govern the earth if only he could control his tongue." The observation can be advanced by stating that the command of one's self is the greatest empire a man could aspire to; and consequently—to be subject to our own passions—is the most grievous slavery. Bad and ignoble rulers throughout history have shown that the man who least governs himself is least fitted to govern others. It is critical to control your existence in a changing world.

The world seems to make way for, and follow, the man who has gotten himself together, who knows where he is going, how to get there, and how to turn a remark into a felicitous phrase. When the going gets tough, the man in control of self gets going. His power is derived from organized and intelligently directed knowledge about (1) the components of his mind and body at any age, disease, illness, and diminished income; and (2) mankind's basic fears and emotions. **The class difference between young and those of older age makes it difficult, almost impossible, for elders—even those of dedication, industry, ambition and talent—to often rise above the younger class in a competitive world.**

In developing the principle of self-control, it is self-evident that power is required for the accumulation of wealth, even when stealing from the many to give to the few. Power is also necessary for the retention of wealth. Whenever a wealthy individual or immense corporation fails to exercise self-control, they will experience an erosion of their power base. Often this exertion occurs when either entity loses control of their ego, and when they view themselves and their actions as beyond the law. In almost every instance, the abused power is being used, not by the wealth owners, but by trustees and directors of invested funds, or by holders of the public trust.

If you would aspire to prosper in your bodily gift from God, you must first understand the very essence of life and concentrate on the elimination of the seven basic fears. In time, we hate that which we often fear.

Psalm 23

The LORD is my shepherd; I shall not want.
He maketh me to lie down in green pastures;
He leadeth me beside the still waters.
He restoreth my soul; He leadeth me in the paths of
   righteousness for His name's sake.
Yea, though I walk through the valley of the shadow of death,
I will fear no evil; for Thou art with me;
Thy rod and Thy staff, they comfort me.
Thou preparest a table before me in the presence of mine
   enemies;
Thou anointest my head with oil; my cup runneth over.
Surely goodness and mercy shall follow me all the days of my
   life; and I will dwell in the house of the LORD forever.

The Power of Prayer – *Does God Really Answer?*

"I was rescued from the lion's jaws." - 2nd Timothy 4:17

Author, Ben Sherwood writes in his best-selling book. *The Survivors Club* about a young woman who was attacked in the wilderness by a mountain lion and who called out to God for her miraculous survival. He also reports on the survival of a man whose life was miraculously saved from both of the terror attacks on the World Trade Center in New York City, and who attributed his survival to his abiding faith and fulfilling appeal to God for his rescue in each occasion.

Do people's beliefs influence their mental and physical well-being? Apparently so — because Sherwood's research shows that people who go to church regularly live about seven years longer than those who do not attend services in the House of God. Studies on intercessory prayer (others praying for the survival or benefit of loved ones) can also bring physical and/or mental healing. However, if the person (or persons) to whom the prayers are directed is determined to die — for whatever reason — the prayers could be mentally blocked. When evil forces take control of peoples' lives— such as the destiny of Jews in Nazi concentration camps—survival beyond celestial power is left to peoples' hard work, determination, skill, intelligence, luck, a will to take risks, and belief in the *Bible*.

The *Bible* teaches us to forgive and forget. **And hatred is one of the seven negative emotions, along with revenge, unrighteous anger, envy, greed, fear, and superstition.** The Lord forgave you, so you must learn to forgive others if you wish to reach the pearly gates. (Colossians 3:13)

1. THE FEAR OF DYING

Gerontology scientists reveal that dying of "old age" is a fallacy—that human entity factually ends because of the acute failure of human organs. Darwin said that life was a product of nature—a species of the ape, and that only death was a certainty. Copernicus said that man was no longer the son of God—that he was condemned to death from the hour of his birth. Life has often been likened to energy which, along with matter, cannot be destroyed. Our existence on earth can be demolished; but, as with energy, life also changes form, beginning with a germ cell, emerging through birth, and seemingly ending with death. However, death, it can be argued, is merely a transition stage, wherein, unlike energy, no new form is transfigured. If your soul lives on after death, then surely your soul does not age. You possess eternal youth. Some theorists on aging suggest that we possess hereditary lives after death that exhibit—through newly-born human beings—transformable soul-like characteristics from previous lives that can help or hinder individual progress on the stage of each existential life. This theory supports compassionate reasons for us to nurse and enrich the immortality of the soul through the goodness of our thoughts and actions— a postulate of Christian liturgy urging believers to seek eventual habitat in Heaven. This argument could defeat any theoretical discussion of reincarnation, a questionable spiritual concept that could, in the essence of perceived truth, grossly overpopulate the planet, since every person on earth is—in terms of this theory—born again, resulting in still another body form packed into a crowded world. Of course, many New Age apostates could argue that there are Otherworld realms beyond our "Planet God."

If this theoretical transition of soul transfer from old body to new body does not occur, then what remains after death is a long and abiding sleep; and sleep is not one of mankind's basic fears. If you fear a fiery Hell, or the Devil himself, the conversion to, and sincere practice of, the Christian faith can assure you of eternal salvation, blessed by presence with the Lord in an open sesame to the Elysian Fields, and joined by beloved soul mates departed from the earth.

Successful agers—**pursuing a Christ-like life**—have, throughout history, expected to die; so when departure time on earth arrived at their deathbed, they were cured of any age concerns and had no earthly fears, being in the comfort of their Father in Heaven. It does not pay well for the children of God to spend every remaining day on earth reading obituary columns when the *Bible* is readily at hand for their guidance into eternity.

2. FEAR OF GROWING OLD

Old age, for many of us, may seem a long way off; but when the yellow leaves of life appear, it will be too late to do anything about it. Control of self means the conquering of this fear by preparing for the eventuality and enjoyment of the days outworn. Even when such chants of "HOPE and CHANGE" now appear to be whispers of an idealistic scam—and you are still broke—you will not want to abandon your faith for the pursuit of false hope. The world once heralded Kant and the citadel of atheism. And to what end? When you see an old man or woman of good humor—friendly, equable, and content—you can be sure that their youth was wisely spent. Patience, justice, and generosity were among the coins they placed on life's counter. They do not try to return their spent years for the fresh merchandise of youth. They do not fear a sunset. They are like the evening of a fine day.

On average, out of every 100,000 people born in the U.S.A., about 60% live to 80 years of age. (*Internet market* data); and a 60-year-old woman has a 50/50 chance of living to 85; while a 65-year-old man has a 50/50 chance of living another 17 years. (*Society of Actuaries*). Instead of dreading the clock of old age, we should be mellowed by the stealing hours of time. Our 70's, 80's and 90's are like a second childhood. An award-winning playwright and author, age 82, said, "I am far happier than I was in my 60's. I was frightened of old age. Now it's here. I'm happy with it."

The surest sign of old age is loneliness; but be careful in your choice of the company you keep at the top of Good Old Age. Throughout life we are often drawn to people and things we fear. And our gift of age from God could reach a hundred years for many of us. In a good number of retirement communities, the topic of conversation may consistently be drawn to complaints about bad old age—discussions that could challenge your thought processes, pushing you into bouts of anxiety and despair. And a 54-year Harvard study of aging males revealed that the key to happiness was love, hands down; and the projection is that by 2036 there will be an age increase of one per year.

When addressing the fear of old age, after experiencing weakness following a strenuous walk, St. Paul of the Cross said in a letter, "I was more tired from my little walk than I used to be after walking thirty miles. But I am content with the most Holy Will of God. It is the Lord who allows many of His children to live to an old age, and, if this is your calling from Him, it can serve a larger purpose; it can also benefit you spiritually, as long as you're willing to surrender your will to him."

Plato kept his zeal for self-improvement for over 80 years—a time frame, that for most of us, is the passing luxury of youth.

3. FEAR OF BECOMING ILL

Of extreme concern to agers under attack by lingering and looming sickness is the unhappy prospect of confinement to a nursing home, where you can be thrown into the company of strangers and lose elements of your privacy and basic freedoms. Generally, this issue creates fear for us when we are faced with injurious accidents and physical disabilities; so it is wise for you to (1) exercise and move about regularly; (2) watch your diet; and (3) keep your mind alert with activity, even when you are alone. It is your mind, primarily, that makes your body rich or poor.

Napoleon Hill, in his classic book, *You Can Work Your Own Miracles*, tells of an experiment he conducted during one of his lectures to demonstrate the imaginary physical ailment known as hypochondria. A number of "stooges" were pre-selected by Dr. Hill to approach a "victim" during intermission and inquire about his health. One would rush up and say something such as, "You look pale. Is anything wrong?" Another stooge then came along and insisted that the victim sit down before he collapsed. A third stooge subsequently appeared to confirm the diagnosis. "You look as if you're going to faint. I'd better get you a glass of water." By this time, a crowd would have gathered; and stooge number three would add, "Make room, please. This man needs a place to lie down. He's about to pass out." If the victim was still on his feet, it would not be for too long. The role of the fourth stooge was to grab the victim by the arm and exclaim to all assembled, "Someone call a doctor quick. This man needs attention."

In all cases where the experiment was performed, the "victim" became convinced of his illness. In fact, one young man required hospitalization; and the doctors inherited the difficult task of convincing him that his illness was a psychosomatic disorder brought on by a hoax. Following this incident, Dr. Hill abandoned the experiments. He had proved beyond doubt that ill health can be "willed" on someone by his or her own mind; and the comments and actions of others are not necessarily required to bring this about.

As an elder, I know from personal experience that the horrors of lengthy hospital stays still exist; and the experience can infect some of us with cognitive decline, as reality battles any comforting spiritual and metaphysical thoughts and truths. Notwithstanding to cases of legitimate sickness, ill health can be sort of an early old age that—when taken to an extreme state of conviction—can reflect a lack of confidence in our ability to move on in life. *Common and vulgar people ascribe all ill that they feel to others; people of little wisdom ascribe to themselves; people of much wisdom to no one* – Epictetus.

4. FEAR OF PAIN

Each of us hangs upon a cross of ourselves, and when you grasp this truth, you will be wise. As pointed out earlier, if your pleasure is gathering roses, you soon lose the fear of thorns. Pain seems to stalk pleasure like a shadow. To know pleasure is to know pain; otherwise you would pursue pleasure to your death. Active and pleasurable sports require pain to bring rest; the birth of a child is preceded by pain. Rest and relaxation is nature's way of restoring your energies. Fear of pain (mental and physical) is, of course, different from living with pain; however abnormally-held fears can greatly aggravate those real pains we must learn to live with. A few of the best defenses against abnormal fear of pain, and against fear itself, are a reduction in your emotion levels based on prayer, mindful meditation, empathy, and information on subjects contained in this book. Of course, the horror of pain could be so severe that you feel yourself not quite dead, but not wholly alive; and life has become little more than a recurring belief that your suffering is not death.

A mind out of control with unwarranted fears and inflamed emotions is easy prey for the fangs injecting physical pain. The self-discipline you gain by conditioning your mind for the acceptance of pain will serve you well when pain is to be experienced, and when it actually occurs. Men in the heat of battle, primitive women in childbirth, the early American Indian, all have learned to live with pain beyond what we consider to be human endurance. Football players have at times been hit so hard while carrying the ball toward the goal that they have been classified as unconscious—nature's stop-gap way for pain endurance; yet they push on for a touchdown. How? When interviewed, many of these athletes have stated that, upon being hit, all reality was gone. Their minds could not conceive pain. All that mattered was to reach the goal line ahead. This done, the clouds of emotion appeared, and pain was experienced. At this point, each athlete began to lose control over his own mind—the empire of the brain of which the Creator had given him complete charge.

History has proved that the great and successful leaders of mankind, in all of their endeavors, have mastered the fear of mental and physical pain. If you would emerge from failure in life, you must overcome this fear. Realize, however, that unless your mind is properly conditioned, even the simple toothache will try your strongest power of will. But the sting of pain, like the edge of pleasure, is blunted by the mind long prepared; for the hurt and the balm are diluted by the waters of patience. We scream at the innocent nurse because the scoundrel doctor is unavailable to authorize more pain pills. Who are we to blame? Bitterness is psychological in nature and more easily borne than our agonies from physical pain; thus a strong and well prepared mind will lead to less suffering than those who give way to irritation.

Remember, first, that suffering from life's setbacks, including pain, are not wholly evil—however much we may fear our misfortunes—and second, that pain and loss of material gain are seldom far removed, but that both give strength, and depth, and fruitfulness to one another. Only through the loss of life's pleasures, can God stir up his love for a hungry heart.

5. FEAR OF LOST LOVE AND LONELINESS

There is no creature loves me; and if I die no soul shall pity me. -- Shakespeare

It is said that the fear of lost love is the cause of more murders and suicides than all other reasons combined. It is also believed by many that more enterprise and accomplishments have been thrown to the wind over this fear than all of man's efforts to date. Jesus warned us against the commonest source of our vainest anxieties, the imaginary fear of what may be.

We learn from the treatise of prophets of old that fear of lost love has changed more minds, influenced more people to do wrong, and scared more personalities than all of the despots the world has ever known. And as we advance in life the circle of our pains enlarges, while the number of our friends contracts. Their bright and wrinkled faces are no more—seemingly no one left to tell us we're looking younger. *I alone am left on earth!* You converse with what is above you. But while one finds company only in himself and his pursuits, he cannot be old, whatever his years may be.

To obtain peace of mind, and to begin mastering this fear, you must properly interpret and relate to the following basic law of nature. *When something is taken away from you (love, friends) the seed of an equivalent benefit will be left behind to grow.*

Loneliness strikes at all ages, and it can lead to dementia, Alzheimer's, suicide, and even murder. Your brain can be tricked into believing your actions and demeanor are less hurtful than they really are. Once love is lost, sorrow can bring about reforms over such undesirable traits as arrogance, selfishness, vanity, and self-love (narcissism). An abnormal or unjustified fear about losing the love of those close to you can undo all of your efforts to achieve lasting happiness and success. If you are afraid to address this fear for what it is and accept the falseness of anger, the fear will not fade away. This lack of mental courage can bring about feelings of failure; your work performance and demeanor can be lackluster and substandard; and melancholia can poison your ability to think accurately.

Remember: It is better to have loved and lost than never to have loved at all. – Tennyson

Whether the fear is real or imagined, the result is the same—a loss of control over your own mind; and the floodgates are opened to the Seven Negative Emotions: **Hate, Envy, Greed, Fear, Superstition, Revenge, and Anger.** Consider the four essential components of your life:

1. Physical concerns;
2. Mental attitudes;
3. Social involvements;
4. Spiritual needs

When any of these components is imbalanced, there is disruption in your life. Fear of lost love is an insidious disease that can disrupt a healthy mental attitude, thus impeding progress toward your goals. The other components of your life are burdened by the imbalance. Prolonged anguish can aggravate the wound and cause deterioration of the other three components, thus undermining the very structure of your life. Only when love is actually lost, or your fears established as unfounded, can you begin to shut out the predominance of negative emotions over positive emotions and allow the fresh currents of *desire*, *faith*, *love*, *sex*, *enthusiasm*, *romance*, and *hope*, to enter your life. These positive sentiments flow and recede inversely when reacting to an imbalance in any of the four basic life-long components.

Your living tools for operating your life are: **body**, **brain**, **heart**, and **soul**. These tools work best for you when they are continually refined and maintained in perfect order.

The Seven Positive Emotions are:

1. Desire
2. Faith
3. Love
4. Sex
5. Enthusiasm
6. Romance
7. Hope

The Seven Negative Emotions are:

1. Hate
2. Envy
3. Greed
4. Fear
5. Superstition
6. Revenge
7. Unrighteous Anger

6. FEAR OF BEING POOR

Why is it that they complain too much; that they echo or anticipate Job's wonder why the just suffer so, while the ruthless prosper...?

A rich man once was asked, "Are you afraid you'll ever lose all of your money?" He replied, "Poverty is uncomfortable; I've been there." But the best thing that can happen to a young man is to be tossed overboard to learn to sink or swim on his own. He would then focus on his present crisis rather than troubles ahead; so if he conquers the fear of poverty now, it won't hurt him when he becomes rich.

In this world, you'll find contentment among rich and poor alike; but *he who fears he will be poor can never truly be rich.* It may seem as if the self-made rich of this world were motivated by an intense desire not to become poor. The often-cited quotation, "I've been rich, and I've been poor; but believe me, rich is better," is more an afterthought by aging personages rather than a statement of motivation. Obviously it is better to have money than to be without it and live out of your saddlebag or a home on the street, where more emotional speed bumps will spare you nothing but health set-backs and detours in your flight from adversity.

The self-made rich and successful person views poverty as no more than an unwelcome shadow, certainly not the ghostly apparition of the security-conscious individual who attracts disaster to himself with his own thoughts of ruin. The ancestor to any action—good, bad, or evil—is thought.

The poor can at least revel in their privilege to be happy and unenvied; to be free of analysts and guards; and to take from nature's bounty what the great and wealthy are compelled to purchase in the name of pleasure. As a rule, rich and successful persons do not fear poverty, because this fear is the antithesis of one of the ten basic motives—material gain. It is the want of material things, not obsessive concern about living in the basement of poverty, that spurs individual enterprise. In the daily papers and magazines, and on television news programs, you observe the lives of featured rich and poor alike. The courageous and truly poor of this world certainly do not like their plight; but they don't suffer from a fear of poverty, because they are there already and kindness of the poor to the poor is a saint's mission—riches given out of little—with no thought of return.

I recall shuffling on stage in a line of kids at a school auditorium at Christmas time to receive a gift donated to the poor. I was delighted to receive a wind-up train and tracks; and, as a young teenager, I remember exchanging my art work at school for necessary clothing. Just as the foot is the measure of the shoe, so are the real wants of nature the measure of enjoyment.

7. FEAR OF BEING CRITICIZED

Criticism can be likened, in a poetic way, to an arrow winging straight and true toward a target in the air. You're soaring like an eagle through rolling clouds until struck by the fatal dart. The shaft quivers in your heart while, still, your ambitions, hopes and dreams cry out for greater heights. How great, you feel, must be those feathers which propelled the steel that returns you to your nest—greater, surely, than your own plumage, which now drinks the last drop of blood from your bleeding breast.

Resolve here and now to soar still higher when the real and imagined barbs of criticism strike you in the breast. It is simply not possible to live through the great heights of life when you are burdened with worry over what other people think, do, or say. For example, memory is what makes us young or old; and elders often find it difficult to remember names. Or perhaps you forgot your ATM pin number. Simply be thankful in your Good Old Age that you remembered what an ATM was. Fight off fears of criticism by understanding that humans find it is much easier to be critical than correct, this we learned from "name calling" in past elections.

Remember this about the fear of criticism. In most instances, critics instinctively fear that or whom they do not know: "You're not so great." In real life, people you dislike are often better than the estimate you form of them. We may think of a person as a monster; only to find out later that he or she a real person, perhaps just like you.

Opinions are the cheapest commodities on the face of the earth. If taken in quantity, they will lead to cancer of the soul and undermine your power of will. Criticism, like advice, is freely given away; but watch that you take only what will not destroy you. Somehow life seems to favor those who

1. **know precisely what they want to accomplish, and**
2. **what they do not want to achieve. As you advance in life, you'll be faced down with a wind of criticism. Fear of criticism and shallow goals are found in the swamp of failure, even as we begin to patch up our bodies for Heaven.**

If you hesitate to free yourself, or if you follow the false channels of despair and delusion and drift into disbelief over a beneficent afterlife, you risk spending the remainder of your life on earth trapped in the bogs of misery.

The channel to wealth, independence, and a prosperous life, requires you to set, or reset your goals—not only to reach docks on rivers and tributaries of success on earth—but to sail on to the ocean of peace and happiness in the home of God. If others would think your goals are unreachable or unrealistic; and if they would discourage your attempts with disparaging remarks and conflicting effort, you must press on, or else your fondest hopes and dreams will perish. When you succumb to negative situations, such as excessive criticism and "nagging," you risk altering the chemistry of the brain to where you will lose all ambition and sink deeper into the swamp of failure and distress. Remember that a winner never quits in the face of criticism. **In my comeback, I aimed at stopping a financially disastrous foreclosure by a certain date, making a cash-producing land sale on time; earning a specific amount of money within a specified period; and publishing this book by a certain date. Each goal was gained as I overcame a multitude of obstacles in Good Old Age.**

Conviction of purpose and a burning desire to follow your hopes and dreams are the best weapons against this awesome fear. It can blow away the blossoms, as well as the caterpillars, from your tree of growth—no matter what your age may be. All of your hopes, desires, and plans can fall to earth if your mind becomes weakened by the fear of criticism. **Important: Do not talk to others about your efforts to advance your life for the good. Judge your own improvement; otherwise the firmness of your mind, passions, and affections may crumble, thereby risking the loss of your connection with the subconscious; and you may sacrifice what you have learned and have to start all over in your mission to improve yourself.**

Here is the procedure for nurturing your roots and influencing the achievement of your constantly changing goals as you proceed through life:

1. WRITE OUT A STATEMENT OF YOUR GOALS. This statement will be ineffective against criticism without these six little helpers: "I had six honest serving men; they taught me all I knew. Their names were <u>What</u> and <u>Where</u> and <u>When</u> and <u>Why</u> and <u>How</u> and <u>Who</u>. It is helpful to be specific in your wishes or prayers.

2. DEVELOP AN INTENSE ENTHUSIASM WITHIN YOURSELF OVER THE GOALS YOU'VE REACHED IN LIFE AND/OR YOUR PLANS TO ACHIEVE OTHER GOALS. You must act from the heart on this next point: Don't shut your doors against a setting sun. Get yourself off the couch and welcome the swinging days ahead. Spend less time searching for a shadow life in social media. Sing, dance, talk to yourself; practice, or volunteer your services, until you can feel the breath of achievement, and the fever of reason to utilize whatever talents God has given to you in life, and to enjoy moments of serenity for the gifts of goodness you have passed on to others—this through your efforts and your very existence. Remember, criticism never opened a good show; nor closed down a bad one.

3. REPEAT THE STATEMENT OF GOALS NIGHT AND DAY AFTER EACH OF YOUR "ENTHUSIASM" OR "PRAYER" SESSIONS, BELIEVE THAT YOUR GOALS WILL BE ACTED UPON IN RETURN FOR

SERVICES THAT YOU WILL GIVE, AND ARE GIVING TO OTHERS. EXPRESS GRATITUDE FOR WHAT IS YET TO COME. ASK AND YOU WILL RECEIVE **(See Rule #13)**

To see yourself receiving rewards, and achieving and setting out goals, you must—through commensurate effort—promise and deliver something in return. The undying strength of this goal pact is your insurance against the undermining influence of criticism.

Remember this: The Creator has given you the power of controlling your own mind—notwithstanding the cruelty and brutality of evil and misguided leaders in the world, stifling freedom of thought. Through the blurred fear of criticism, you relinquish this power of mind control to others who may, in turn, successfully direct this power to whatever ends they may choose. Your only limitations are those which you set up in your own mind (through fear) or permit others to establish for you (through criticism).

MONEY LESSON LEARNED: Make your money multiply and work for you. Ready money is Aladdin's lamp.

Chapter 7
S(C)RIPT and FLAME RULE #5
Master the Power of
<u>CONCENTRATION</u>

Andrew Carnegie, the inspiration for Napoleon Hill's classic self-help book, *Think and Grow Rich*, had this to say about the habit of *concentration*: "Concentration is my motto—first honesty, then industry, then persistence." Carnegie, the founder of the company known as U.S. Steel, was, along with Henry Ford, one of the most successful and influential industrialists of his day, as well as one of the world's richest men. *Concentration* and persistence breed genius. If you can get back on your feet after being knocked down a dozen times by failure, you have proved yourself capable of accomplishment beyond the norm.

Thomas Edison failed 10,000 times before inventing the incandescent light. *Concentration* and persistence have (1) lifted mankind to the stars and back; (2) conquered disease; (3) produced awesome weapons of war: and (4) have finally duplicated the process by which the human egg is fertilized.

Intense *concentration* and persistence are the main reasons that records of unbeatable feats of human skill and endurance continue to be broken. These qualities are behind (1) election of our presidents; (2) the success of many major stars in the theater and the arts; (3) the solace of self-made millionaires and billionaires; and (4) the sustenance of all great novelists and other writers. Even in social life, it is persistence which attracts confidence—more than talents and accomplishments. And it is said that a lowly rat, by persistently gnawing through a dyke, could even drown a nation.

Old age has often been touted as an incurable disease. Likewise is the game of golf. Looking back in life, I remember what Sam Snead, the great golfer, said about concentrated effort: "*Concentration* is so important. You have to know that the ball is going into that hole." At the time, Snead had won more regular P.G.A. tournaments than were listed in the Guinness Book of Records for shooting the lowest score in tournament play—an incredible 59! Another sports record-holder from yesteryear was the amazing baseball player, Pete Rose. He applied such a steady and intense effort to win that his hitting streak of 44 straight games captured the imagination and attention of an entire nation.

When he fell short of DiMaggio's magic mark of hitting in 56 consecutive games, Pete Rose went on to proclaim he would *concentrate* on becoming the greatest hitter in baseball. And the legendary basketball coach, Bobby

Knight, fired after 29 years and three national titles at Indiana University, "The General" pressed on in his 60's to become the first Division 1 men's coach to gather 900 career wins.

If you think the powers of *concentration* and persistence are available only to the young great and super great, consider that Rose, Knight, and others like them had to fight serious deficiencies, including aging, to reach the top. Rose had this to say about coming from behind:

"There are a lot of guys with tremendous talent. . . younger guys with more size, speed, and power than I've got—and guys with faster swings, or quicker wrists, and things like that. But I think I get more out of it than any other player in baseball. I get the most out of whatever talent or advantages I have. I don't have a good arm either; but I throw out more runners than anybody else with an arm like mine."

Concentration on the task at hand is critical to success, particularly as we pass fifty, the youth of old age, when we begin to love everything old. Few things are impractical in themselves. More people fail to learn how to grow old than those who lack the means to reach a satisfactory level in their autumn years of life. In school I sat next to Roy Clark, the great county and western music star from the *He Haw* television series of the 70's; and I recall the intense effort and *concentration* he applied to whatever he was doing, be it baseball or "pickin." During his time, he had probably mastered more musical instruments than anyone else in his field. In his early years, winning contests and awards became a habit with him. He simply would not give up. When failure and imminent tragedy stalked him, he *concentrated* the power of his mind toward ridding those shadows from his life.

The incredible powers of *concentration*, nourished and developed, are applied relentlessly toward the achievement of specific goals, and are behind the success of every great person in history. Even past despots and dictators, such as Hitler, were intense thinkers who refused to be dissuaded by more rational, though less intense, thought. As time goes by, our memories have a tendency to slip away from us; and the protection of memory—considered by some to be an element of accumulated genius—can call for a serious hearing. Failure to *concentrate* on our goals and efforts in life can lead to an incurable mental illness as we pass a mid-point in life.

A study from Chicago's Rush University revealed that a group of elderly Catholic sisters had an 89% lower risk of developing Alzheimer's than a comparative group of less conscientious people. Isaac Newton traced back his memory discoveries to unwearied *concentration*; and *concentration's* gift to humanity is acclaimed by mankind for such achievements as building bridges, opening new worlds, and healing diseases.

***Concentration* allowed me to turn $50 in nickels and dimes into a net worth of over 5 million; to dismount as a trail boss and saddle up as a real estate broker—without spending a day as a licensed**

salesman; to rise from selling a mountain top to owning and selling a 5,000-acre mountain range in the D.C. Metro area; and to go from selling, brokering and developing more than 300 square miles of land over four highly-populated states. Following are the three critical steps for pursuing the powers of concentration:

1. **DEFINE AND PURSUE SPECIFIC GOALS**
   Most problems, well-organized and defined, are already partially solved. Move positively once your goals are clearly defined. i.e: increased income; investments, cosmetic or other surgery; changes in habits, lifestyle, career; attitude; social expectations, diet; exercise; education; spirituality, etc.

2. **DEVELOP FAITH**
   Follow the precepts of the Nazarene who said, *"Ask and it will be given to you; seek and you will find; knock and it will be opened to you. For everyone who asks, receives; and he who seeks, finds."* Matthew 7: 7-8
   "For truly I say to you, if you have faith as a grain of mustard seed, you will say to this mountain, (or obstacle) 'Move from here to there,' and it will move; and nothing will be impossible to you." Matthew 17-20

3. **ADOPT A POSITIVE MENTAL ATTITUDE**
   Think success in achieving your goals! A greater part of our happiness or misery depends on our disposition and not on our circumstances. "I can't," is an idea—not fact. Success is achieved and maintained by those who keep trying.

Finally, remember this about the power of *concentration*. Just reading about solutions to problems, and looking at success—at whatever our age—will not bring success in achieving our goals; nor will success come to those who merely understand what they read and perceive about the subject. However, success will seek you out if you act on what you learn about this principle. Age shines out for a purpose in life; for one day you will retire.

MONEY LESSON LEARNED: Let wise men hold money in their heads for you. You keep money in your heart.

Chapter 8
S(C)RIPT AND FLAME RULE #6
Act To <u>COOPERATE</u> With Others

The great industrialist, Willard F. Rockwell, Jr. carried a quote from a psychologist in this wallet. It reads, "Don't forget that every human being has this motto on his chest: I want to be important". In struggling with advancing age and success, remember that the whole (your life) is equal to the sum of all the parts (those around you) and is greater than any one of the parts (you). The most damaging weakness of elders who have been friendly all of their life is to forget they are no longer congenial. If you expect to walk off the ball field a winner, you must have the *cooperation* of your players. Don't play negative, defensive, and emotional games with them or walk over them. Remember, you cannot pat the back of a person whom you are required to defeat.

A humorous story to emphasize this point comes to mind:

A pretty young lady walked into a sporting goods store and ordered equipment for a baseball game, including a baseball, a bat, a catcher's mitt, and a catcher's mask.

"Are you sure you want all of these?" asked the salesman. The girl nodded. "Yes, I do. My boss is getting older. He said if I'd play ball with him we'd get along fine."

Friendship is said to be the wine of life; yet it is full of dregs. Many elders live solitary lives disconnected from their family. They depend on friends to the point where each party can seem necessary for the other. Mere survival from isolation becomes a critical issue in life, particularly when sickness and poverty strike the soul—when agers have left their purest form and are no longer children.

A true friend can be like two souls in the same body, even to the point of extending life spans and showing the rightfulness of Heaven in the face of groans, pities, and cold-heartedness on earth. Compassion is an emotion of which we should never be ashamed; however many pastors, social workers, and counselors, suffer tears of sympathy by listening with deep concern to a steady stream of woeful discontent from distressed humans in their care. We learn from them that there is a subservient element of humanity that is a direct reflex of distress.

Consider the volunteer workers in ghettos and refugee camps, missionaries, and other servants of God; they gain nothing better from the (1) modern world and its vision of comfort without effort; (2) pleasure without pain of creation; and (3) sterilization against the thought of death—all shadows of life they do not wish to pursue. The high degree of affection served by these compassionate people tends to create negative vibrations that can offset positive motivations. If taken to extremes, the merited effort of those with the fairest heart can be defeated, dismissing compassion for the mean and miserable.

COPING WITH STRESS AND UNITY

Retirees living with their children and dealing with upended family dynamics can find themselves at the center of arguments about their presence—quarrels often related to petty causes springing up daily in the household. From being even-tempered, cheerful and active, older adults may become moody, lethargic, and irritable. The elder who deserts the contest—and lets the discourse fall—can exhibit a helpful degree of wisdom—a commendable attribute noted in sages of old. But patient endurance has its limits, and a serious variable may erupt as to what a compassionate family is to do with the *unruly* aged-youth in the house. Given this uncomfortable situation, you—the stumbling retired person lurking about upstairs—would certainly want to be in control of your own circumstances. That is why, *even before retirement* you would need cooperation with other players in this game of life, and certainly reason enough to learn and practice the **16 Rules** given to you in this book. Age does not depend upon years but upon temperament and health. Some of us are born old, and some never grow so. You will find much to say about unity of one to another in the *Bible*.

In the average business endeavor, a relatively small percentage of people end up shouldering responsibility for the success of the enterprise. The same state of affairs applies when managing a household. The others involved are physically there, though their minds and spirits may be elsewhere. Some may take from the circumstances more than they contribute.

Your success is dependent upon your identification and proper handling of the producers, rather than the reducers, though emotional concerns can tip the scales in family situations. In an enterprise, surround yourself with people who have the talents you lack, and pay them well. In friendships, you owe them nothing. Success in personal affairs and in business is a *cooperative* effort and is seldom achieved by managers and partners operating for and unto themselves. The lack of harmonious coordination of effort is the main cause of practically every human failure.

Think of the Allies at the beginning of World War II. Their ranks were badly split by dissention and factionalism. Only a supreme organizer and manager of the *cooperative* spirit could pull them together to defeat the Axis powers in Europe and North Africa. General George C. Marshall—himself a great leader of armies—selected Eisenhower, a young military officer whose forte had been getting people to work together toward a common goal. He had never before commanded armies in the field; but he was a genius at organizing cooperative effort.

Think of Sir Edmund Hillary on Mount Everest, falling to his death, only to be saved by his trusted Sherpa guide, Tenzing Norgay. Norgay knew the crevasses on Everest; he knew its best campsites, its peaks. He was the best man for the job. Without him, Hillary would never have reached the top.

Consider the prosperous times of the great Republican leader, President Ronald Reagan, who rallied a contentious Democrat Congress behind his efforts to repair a divided and economically-ravaged country and convinced our strongest enemy, the Soviet Union, to stand down. And remember the happy marital alliance between Reagan and his wife, Nancy. Could he have reached this fortuitous level of *cooperation* without her? Harmony with others is critical today. Over a quarter of marriages now end in divorce. The list goes on to our internet days, with the famous names of those who used *cooperative* effort to build great and profitable companies: Jobs, Gates, Trump, Buffet, Rockefeller, Carnegie...

These stories point up the need for you to assemble or maintain a team of *cooperative* and enthusiastic people around you if you hope to reach the pinnacles of happiness, while avoiding the quicksand of life. Napoleon Hill referred to the assembling of such a group as forming a "Mastermind Alliance". You can create such an alliance even if you start late in life, with just you, or with your family, in a business—on the web, or in a garage.

Such an alliance is responsible for the success of the world's most famous hotel and motel chain—Holiday Inns, Inc. The founder, Kemmons Wilson, when asked about the principal reason for his success replied, "I guess I'm just smart enough to surround myself with the necessary brains and technical know-how that I don't have." Wilson, named by the *London Sunday Times* as one of the thousand most important men of the 20th century, never hesitated to point out in his speeches that his success was largely due to other people, often exemplary and heroic figures of the past.

Another famous practitioner of the "Master-mind" alliance theory was Henry Ford. Once, during a libel suit instituted by Ford against a Chicago newspaper, the defense attorney opened Mr. Ford to scorn and ridicule over his lack of formal education. "Listen," Ford told the lawyer, "I have not built this company by cluttering up my mind with general knowledge just so I can answer foolish questions. By pushing the right button on my desk, I can bring to my office an expert to answer any question I want about my business in the most profitable manner for all concerned."

Let us now make up a mind game. Behind the men who have built up fortunes with the help of others, stand six indispensable guards, all usually present in the subconscious mind of these men. These guards—of the past and present—are at the disposal of the leader of the "Master-mind" group and are principally responsible for his leadership role. The absence of any of these guards can weaken and destroy the alliance; so you will want to keep them in hand on the age-old table of hard times. *"What would they do to solve my problem,"* I ask? I chose for my imaginary cabinet—in the order of their attached roles—(1) a world-renowned historic writer; (2) an acclaimed black doctor; (3) a famous evangelist; (4) a notable businessman; (5) a sainted woman; and (6) a revered U.S. President of the past. (See Appendix 3g)

1. **THE GUARD OF MENTAL PEACE**

Progress in age brings us back with a fondness to all that is fresh in the early dawn of youth. Call on him to steer you away from taking illicit and questionable actions and to purge your mind of the seven negative emotions: **Hate, Envy, Greed, Fear, Superstition, Revenge, and Anger.**

2. **THE GUARD OF GOOD HEALTH**

He who has health has hope, and he who has hope has everything. He protects one of life's great riches. Without this guard, you cannot effectively lead; for no person will long follow suffering and the specter of death.

3. **THE GUARD OF FAITH AND HOPE**

Faith is the substance of things hoped for, the evidence of things not seen. He keeps the spiritual path open for you and shows you how—through prayer and autosuggestion—you can make direct and immediate contact with Infinite Intelligence. This guard shows you the way to a positive mental attitude and helps you to avoid battering the gates of Heaven with storms of prayers.

4. **THE GUARD OF FINANCIAL SUCCESS**

This guard will offer you Aladdin's Lamp, aglow with ready money, wisdom, knowledge, and power. He keeps money worries away from you by "balancing your books." He is responsible for seeing that you give something of equal value for all monies received and expected.

5. **THE GUARD OF LOVE**

He who loves guards, is well guarded. He helps you to lead everyone you meet onto a higher plane than when you found them—to do unto others as you would have them do unto you. He makes you understand that you can never speak boldly of yourself without loss, for your accusations will always be believed, your praises never.

6. **THE GUARD OF WISDOM**

We become wiser by adversity, and often by age. This guard is responsible for the "mustering" of the other guards. His principal duty is to exchange failure and unpleasant circumstance for commensurate benefits. He reminds you that people relate themselves to one another in whatever jobs, capacities, or activities to which they are associated because of a motive or motives. Without this guard, you may forget that there can be no permanent human relationship based upon an indefinite or vague motive, or upon no motive at all. A widow or woman in retirement, for example, may be presumed by family and friends to be lonely and sad, when, in fact, she is happiest in the shadow of her work or manly loving heart—a clear motive for wanting to be alone and not a vagueness of *cooperation* with others.

> *Cooperation* does everything when it is perfect. It satisfies desires, simplifies needs, foresees wishes, and becomes a constant fortune.
>
> The desire to be great—to be recognized, and to have riches and personal power—is a healthy desire; but when a person claims their greatness to the world, it is an indication that they have left their ego unguarded, that their pride has taken possession of them.

Friends and associates will soon abandon the person who boldly proclaims that they are the sole master of the situation at hand, for it is evident that they shield some fear or have an inferiority complex. When you reach out for cooperation, remember that one hand alone cannot applaud.

MONEY LESSON LEARNED: **Cooperate with others to own your own home. Keep money lenders away from your door.**

> "Therefore all things whatsoever ye would that men should to to you, do ye even so to them."
>
> - Matthew 7:12

> "I was hungry and you gave me food,
> I was thirsty and you gave me drink,
> I was a stranger and you welcomed me,
> I was naked and you clothed me,
> I was sick and you visited me,
> I was in prison and you came to me" ......
>
> "Inasmuch as you have done it to the least of my brethren you have done it unto me".
>
> - Matthew 25: 30-36; 40

The above example of human compassion was a spiritually-gifted reality to me at a time when I was down and needed to be lifted up!

Chapter 9
SC(R)IPT and FLAME RULE #7
Practice the Golden RULE

There appears to be a no more valid rule for mankind to live by than the Golden Rule. Nevertheless, a lot of fun has been poked at this age-old saying. Take the story of the mother scolding her young daughter after overhearing her and a few friends plotting revenge on a playmate following a fight. The mother kindly took the young conspirator in tow and admonished her, "It seems to me you're going to do to Mary just what you don't want her to do to you. I don't think this is the Golden Rule—is it?

"Well, mama, said the youngster, "the Golden Rule is all right for Sunday; but for me I'd rather have an eye for an eye and a tooth for a tooth."

Obviously, if you sow actions based on the "eye for an eye" attitude, so shall you reap a wrong habit. Sow wrong habits, and you reap bad character. Sow bad character and reap a dark destiny. **Behind all of our actions are the TEN BASIC MOTIVES:**

1. SELF-PRESERVATION
2. LIFE AFTER DEATH
3. FREEDOM OF BODY AND MIND
4. RECOGNITION OF SELF-EXPRESSION
5. MATERIAL GAIN
6. EMOTION OF LOVE
7. EMOTION OF FEAR
8. EMOTION OF SEX
9. EMOTION OF ANGER
10. EMOTION OF HATE

Behind most rich and successful persons lies a full understanding of these basic motives. Ideally—considering the fact that the mind is the one and only thing over which the Creator has provided control for us (and this mentality happens to be self-control)—we would seek to master the substance and tone of these ten basic motives and to use them only for the good they will offer for us to cope with earthly affairs. Using Jesus Christ as the supreme example of one whose motives were beyond suspect, we can, at best, strive to emulate his example when evaluating our motives.

SCRIPT AND FLAME

Jesus Christ is the greatest motivator the world has ever known. His example sets the standard for success in its true form. He is the ultimate practitioner of the Golden Rule. When He spoke, people listened and believed in what he said and preached. His followers were legions in size. Even Pontius Pilate hesitated to disclaim Jesus' mission on earth or to question His motives. Only a few high and corrupt officials among His own people condemned Him, this for reasons of their personal gain.

Now, as in those ancient days, our society uses money as the medium of exchange. **Money is power. And, like power, money can be used for good or evil.** You're reading this book because I claim that the techniques and principles explained here can help you prosper, not only in your financial affairs, but in your future that is purchased by the present. In your quest for success and a contented life, you must not lose sight of the Golden Rule.

An aid to this end is a thorough understanding of the Ten Basic Motives. You'll want to memorize these points of reason and to be true to their meaning. You should be aware of your motives, and the reasoning of others at all times, and strive to recognize the true motives beyond your intents, and the actions of others. **Remember that all thoughts are ultimately translated into their material counterparts. Through the miracle of the human mind, you can determine your own destiny and free yourself from undesirable motives by proper observance of disbelief, morality, and physical reality.**

MORAL HIGH GROUND

The seeds of political correctness often sprout up like weeds in the minds of many "establishment elites," and, throughout the media, forming a steady current of bias and mind control. The stream of God-given redemption mandates then becomes a swamp as errant strivers among us try to pivot away from past and perhaps sinful behavior.

God's grant of free thinking to His children has become a blatant hoax to many unbelievers of the Gospel and "holier than thou" establishment insiders who outwardly condemn controversial social graces and "despicable" moral attitudes and actions that many among them secretly embrace and support, often with no discernable remorse. Redemption is no longer a *get-out-of-jail-free* card for so-called "lewd and crude" upstart buffoons labeled unfit by the self-righteous among us, who claim they can better serve us all with their buckets of failure, despair, and spoiled benefits. Now our falsehoods including past sexual abuse and misbehavior are often legitimized, and a designated low-horse person can be unfairly bridled in his or her persona stall of the day by a debatable headline or news alert. Redemption by the grace of God is available to those true believers who confess their sins and repent.

We are—in social high-horse theory—tied forever to the hitching post of our past; and it is often overly promulgated in the media, and supported by political and social elites—that there will be no prospect of forgiveness for perceived mistakes and misfortunes of the past without approval from an obscure jury of media surrogates. Taking an example from real life—an overplayed expression of the basic negative motive, Anger, following the conclusion of a contested political debate or contest—can develop into a short-term madness, assaulting the victim, and breaking their thought process into pieces, while destroying supporters of the victim. What is done is done. We may not forget; but we can learn to control our anger.

You've heard the saying, "Actions speak louder than words." Remember also, that it is not so much what you say as it is your TONE and MANNER to slights, verbal injuries, alleged unfairness, or imagined fears and anxieties with suspect motivation. You are not advised to call for eye-for-eye revenge.

Remember these key motivational points:

1. **SELF-PRESERVATION** You are not entitled to live at the expense of others.

2. **LIFE AFTER DEATH** Most of the world's religions believe in eternal life.

3. **FREEDOM OF BODY AND MIND** These gifts are grants from the Creator.

4. **SELF EXPRESSION** It is given to everyone; but not at the expense of harming or always blaming others.

5. **MATERIAL GAIN** Share with others. That which remains multiplies.

6. **LOVE** Love is the greatest defense against the spears of hate and anger, and a skillful tool to open the hearts of others.

7. **FEAR** Once overcome, fear will be turned into faith, and this assurance will return to you the possession of your mind, opening ways to grant your desires and reject any negative wishes.

8. **SEXUALTY** The cup of sensual pleasure should never be drained to the bottom, for there is always poison in the dregs.

9. **ANGER** The fire you kindle for your enemy can burn yourself more than him.

10. **HATE** Hatred is active, while envy is passive dislike; There is just one step from envy to hate.

MONEY LESSON LEARNED: He that wants money, means, and content is without three good friends. Provide for your future and that of your family.– *Shakespeare*

Chapter 10
SCR(I)PT AND FLAME RULE #8
USE YOUR IMAGINATION

Imagination, as it is often misunderstood, is a characteristic element of the mind, manifesting itself in such image-building powers as fantasy and dreaming. To build and maintain success—to which the creative process is essential—you must understand that imagination is not only a quality, but also a faculty—a skill developable through action or practice. Memory is the first faculty of the mind that flourishes and the first that dies. So to prosper in the bubble of life, you'll never want to stop learning—to use the coinage of your brain to imagine. Remember! *Imagination* never dies, and success makes success as money makes money. If, then, you can make *IMAGINATION* work for you, it can logically be termed a servant of your will. If you do not call upon this servant, it will grow lazy and inefficient, leaving your mind filled with cobwebs and open to wrong conclusions and false premises. Keep your *imagination* sane and in communion with Heaven.

At age 81, when others were *imagining* retirement trips, I was imprisoned in a hospital bed *imagining* my 20-year plan for the rest of my life, as revealed in this book. At this same time, some political leaders were faced with spears of ridicule and fiery headlines because of their past miscues and blunders, media bias had imagined them as false leaders, crooks and corrupt cronies out to destroy lives and tear apart a great country—a bastion of freedom and liberty that had (1) become a hopeless nation of greed, prejudice and intolerance, or (2) a deteriorating socio-economic and political machine.

Of course, the map on our faces shows days outworn, and we begin to patch up our bodies for Heaven. Yet, as the twilight of our youth fades away, we can still see perennial stars on earth like Billy Graham, Irving Berlin, Helen Hayes, and Grandma Moses, whose *imagination* and creative endeavors defied their age. Poets and dramatists, of course, have acquired *imagination* through performance and practice. And successful men of business use the power of imagination to build commerce, though the products of their labor are dissimilar. In the investment banking business, for example, it is natural for people to be money conscious, since money is their product; wealth is constantly in their thoughts. It is imagined that, as the investment grows, the more money the investor will have.

Consider Shakespeare's poem on *imagination*:

And as imagination bodies forth the form (problems) the poet's pen (successful person) turns to shape (definition and solution) and gives to them airy nothing (opportunity — a local habitation and a means to an end). Such tricks has strong imagination that if he would but apprehend some joy (riches; comfort), it comprehends some bringer of that joy (your services); Or in the night some imagining, some fear (7 basic fears); how easy is a bush (obstacle) supposed a bear (defeat)?

Interpretation: The successful person identifies problems and seeks solutions that lead to opportunity and goal setting toward riches and comforts, while dispensing with *imaginary* fears and overcoming obstacles that would offer only defeat.

A Seattle Longitudinal Study reveals that (1) a person's mind power begins to dwindle in their mid-60's; (2) that the average person's vocabulary is generally stabilized until their 70's; and that (3) a brain can shrink up to 25% over a lifetime. New data shows that mental acuity at age 85 is a draw from the deck of genetics. The Study further contends that many deaths attributed to Alzheimer's disease may have been misdiagnosed.

W. Clement Stone, the famous success motivator, author, multi-millionaire, and philanthropist, lived to be 100. In his time, Stone parlayed $100 in savings into an insurance empire. He suggested in his books and lectures that your *imagination* should first be utilized toward reducing your past successes into a formula (preferably written). When failure comes around, you can then take out your stores of success knowledge and tell failure to get lost. Stone said, "Aim for the moon. Thinking will not overcome fear, but action will. With a positive mental attitude, failure is a learning experience, a rung on the ladder—a plateau at which to get your thoughts in order and prepare to try again." Stone attributed the thrust of his success to an imaginary cabinet of dynamic and famous personalities who, in his mind, advised him when called upon. The *imaginary* sessions were so effective that he dropped the procedure for several months, feeling the mind power generated in the sessions could take him out of his senses. He soon reinstated the process and entered Good Old Age as a billionaire.

I have used my imagination in this chapter to reduce certain proven success principles into a workable formula to successfully follow a righteous road past the end of life. The key words of "SCRIPT" and "FLAME" are products of my *imagination* and examples of how this faculty, or servant of your mind, can be made to work for you in facing the challenges ahead.

In 1962, Sam Walton, a young man from a modest farming family, founded Wal-Mart Stores, Inc., which grew to be the world's largest corporation by revenue, as well as the biggest private employer in the world. Walton had this to say about *imagination*: "I have always driven to innovate, to take things beyond where they've been." Walton succeeded because he believed all he said. He died at 74, having climbed the tallest mountains of business throughout his later years.

Napoleon said that imagination rules the world, and he acted upon this premise until his downfall. How many stars in the theater and the arts were projected into the filament largely through boundless *imaginations* that saw no limit on their talents and abilities? How many enduring Broadway musicals would be idle story lines if it were not for imagination?

Disbelievers in the divinity of Christ have said that Jesus had the greatest *imagination* of anyone who ever lived—He imagined He was the son of God. They believe that the universe is an imperceptible God who connects everything in a metaphysical world. Yet they readily accept the fact that all of history is incomprehensible without Christ.

Before World War II, a rocket ship to the moon was clearly a fantasy to those on earth, until science paid its debt in 1969 to human *imagination* and visualization. In 1941, General MacArthur was in Australia, humiliated, and forced out of the Philippines by the Japanese, who had sunk our naval force in Hawaii. We were left with a super bathtub navy and a ferocious paper air force to defend the entire Pacific. There was no evidence that our nation could recover from the devastation. MacArthur said from his guts, "I shall return; I repeat, I shall return" when there was no credible evidence that our nation could recover from the devastation. And the *Bible* says, **"Where there is no vision, the people perish."**

It is wiser to count your age from your last success rather than from your most recent failure. William Danforth, in his famous self-help book, *I Dare You*, tells the story of Henry Ford and his belief in the power of imagination, and why you should stay young in your thought processes. There was the time when Ford wanted to obtain unbreakable glass for his new car models. His "experts" told him it couldn't be done. Ford replied, "Bring me younger men of *imagination* who know no reason why unbreakable glass cannot be made. I want ambitious fellows around me who *imagine* nothing is impossible." **Ford soon had his unbreakable glass.**

All of us are *imaginative* in some form or another, for images (and belief) breed desire, often wrongful. Desire, of course, is the inspiration for Action. When developing the success principle of *Imagination*, it is necessary for you to remember this about desire, lest your *imagination* carry you away. **Desires defeat their own purposes, should they be too many, too confusing, or unrealistic.**

SCRIPT AND FLAME

The development and cultivation of imaginative effort toward reaching goals (specific, obtainable, and rightful) can often precede the acquisition of those skills and techniques to reach those ends. Imaginative effort in the pursuit of specific goals also requires you to become knowledgeable about any new and changing field of expected accomplishment; but you should not forget that the wisest among us may always learn something from the humblest laborer, and that education offered to us in colleges and universities is academic in nature, largely having no practical application in real life, and is certainly not the main foundation of success in life.

The cultural change into the computer age during the 1980s obviously caused older folks to recognize that "I am not what I used to be." And it is simply not enough to imagine yourself as a great and rich person, without getting skills and knowledge of your new activity field. A characteristic of eccentric persons is a runaway imagination. People who have imagination without learning have no wings or feet.

While in pursuit of this learning, remember the importance of money and environment in pursuing success. It is foolhardy to imagine yourself (1) a great explorer without going to those regions that need exploring; (2) if your age and physical abilities are unlikely to be up to the task at hand, and; (3) if you have limited funds for your efforts. Actors and actresses who want to become famous go to New York and Los Angeles. Each is a Mecca for television and movies; and both are challenging environments for mid-life folks with tiny purses and thin wallets. And if you can imagine yourself as a rich and successful entrepreneur in real estate, it is best to first get training in the profession—which has no age limit—and acquire a measure of capital if you plan to be a real estate investor.

MONEY LESSON LEARNED: Cultivate the talent, training and assistance you need to increase your ability to earn. Be specific in your goals and aspirations.

Chapter 11
SCRI(P)T and FLAME RULE #9
Develop a Pleasant PERSONALITY

The development and maintenance of a pleasant personality requires, first, the building of character; because no change of circumstances can repair a defect in this personal quality. And since we are largely the product of our individual environments, we measure character by different yardsticks. Assuming, however, that the ultimate test of character strength is found in the life of Jesus Christ, and that great figures such as Lincoln, Washington, and Jefferson, are supreme examples of persons with strength of character, you can, through self-discipline, stimulate improvement.

Of course, goodness of character is always attractive when looking back on great figures in life; but goodness, when it has man in its grasp, can destroy his persona; and it has been said that, "No man is a hero to his valet; nor a saint to his brother; for either the brother knows too much, or else his standard utterly excludes all defects." As we trip and stagger through time, we like to review our past achievements and play down our faults, often storing them away in the basement of our memory.

A Mayo Clinic study showed that 1,800 undereducated elders could delay dementia by engaging in activities such as board games, reading, and music. Journalist Barbara Bradley Hagerty explains in her book, *Life Reimagined*, the theory of neuroplasticity—that new brain cells can grow to your last day.

Every person has three character traits: (1) that which he or she exhibits; (2) that which the individual actually has, and; (3) that which the person thinks they have. As we age, these components appear to coalesce into one and can be observed by others to be a singular characterization of an individual. A pleasant personality cannot be manufactured like a smile, a middle-age crisis act, or a handshake, to help you make money off of other people. Faulty motivation, like weak mortar, will lead to the building of a false structure. If you are advancing in age, you would want something in your personality, except your years, to produce as proof that your name will be written in Heaven.

Let's take a peek in the *Bible* to see what it says about the character of those who may dwell with the Lord:

> *He who walks uprightly, and does what is right, and speaks truth from his heart; He who does not backbite with his tongue, Nor does evil to his neighbor, Nor does he take up a reproach against his friend, in whose eyes a vile person is despised; But he honors those who fear the LORD; He who swears to his own hurt and does not change; He who does not put out his money as usury; Nor does he take a bribe against the innocent. He who does these things shall never be moved.* **PSALM 15. A Psalm of David**

If you would sell yourself to others, you will find that a flawed personality repels, rather than attracts. Emerson said, "The only way to have a friend is to be one." And since there is always room for improvement in every person on earth, there is no reason why you have to be stuck for the rest of your life with certain character flaws. The following story emphasizes this point.

A turtle was on his way across the river when he encountered a scorpion:

"Help! I can't swim any longer, I'll drown," cried the scorpion. "Are you crazy?" said the turtle. "If I help you, you'll sting me, and I'll die."

"What a foolish thought," gasped the scorpion. "If I were to sting you, I would surely go down with you. Now where is the logic in that?"

"Sounds right," said the turtle. The scorpion climbed on the turtle's back, and halfway across the river he gave the Good Samarian turtle a mighty sting on the neck. As they both sank to the bottom, the turtle resignedly said, "Would you mind telling me something before I die? You said it wasn't logical for you to sting me. Why, then, did you do it?"

"It's not about logic," the drowning scorpion sadly replied, "It's just my character."

Several lessons are to be learned here. **First**, it is wise as you flee from youth to flood your life with laughter; **Second**, don't be afraid to ask for assistance; and **Third**, disassociate yourself from persons of questionable character before you can begin to sweeten the sourness of aging in this life and beyond into celestial bliss. A helpful aid to these ends is to select persons of strong and cheerful character—real or imagined—whom, because of your admiration for them, you can mentally invite into a sort of cabinet. These will be your silent advisors on matters of character—individuals selected from real life, historical or contemporary figures, famous or obscure personalities, friends, relatives, casual acquaintances who—at appropriate and lonely moments—can be assembled in your mind and asked for advice.

These are people you admire and respect. They can be your heroes. How do you suppose these advisors would handle the problem at hand?

This kind of fantasizing may seem a bit strange to you at first; but, believe me, it works. You can sweeten and strengthen character and begin developing a more pleasing personality—even in your lonely room—by installing such a cabinet in your mind. Talk to your cabinet in private, as you would to God in prayer. Begin to visualize yourself as being in possession of their best qualities. Confirm to yourself, both orally and in writing, that you are becoming more virtuous. Ben Franklin kept a little book where he duly recorded his daily faults as well as his virtues.

But, you say, you don't know where to begin. You may know of only two or three people whom you genuinely admire. Maybe you don't even know them personally. You may have only heard of their good and noble deeds—this from books, television, magazines, word of mouth, or social media. Perhaps they are dear to you and have passed from this life. The answer is to start with them. Return to **Rule #6** listing the six˙ invisible guards who support the men who have built up great fortunes with the help of others.

Remember this: You can have a strong character and still have a lousy personality; but your chance of influencing others are greatly diminished by the imbalance. Consequently, your ability to secure wealth and/or contentment in the autumn of life is jeopardized. You want to build character with the ancillary benefit of strengthening your personality. Begin by talking to your imaginary advisors. Affirm to yourself that you are becoming more like them every day. **Remember, you'll need a qualified advisor for each of the following six posts: Mental Peace, Good Health, Faith and Hope, Financial Success, Love, and Wisdom.**

Acknowledging the power of prayer given to Christ in Heaven and on earth, here are sample historic and contemporary personalities a successful ager might choose as imaginary advisors. Blessed Mother Teresa, Napoleon Hill, Jesse Owens, Billy Graham, Norman Vincent Peale, Ronald Reagan, Steve Jobs, Warren Buffett, Mahatma Gandhi, Albert Schweitzer, Winston Churchill, William Shakespeare, Martin Luther King, or Abraham Lincoln.

One of the first observations you may make about this group of famous personalities is the fact that they have all influenced a great number of people in a very positive way—they are leaders, all possessing such essential leadership qualities as self-confidence, self-sacrifice, morals, paternalism, initiative, decision making, fairness, and courage. Another observation is that these individuals are masters of self-control—and their spirit never dies.

If you would base the strength of your personality on what these exemplary figures have to say, and if you would make it a habit today of making their thoughts your thoughts, you would begin to resemble them tomorrow. Remember Napoleon Hill's famous axiom, **"Whatever the mind of man can believe, it can achieve."** Your imaginary cabinet of advisors will only work for you if you believe deeply and sincerely that such mind power is possible. Obviously this cabinet of advisors will not always be called upon by you as a group—but predominately on a one-to-one basis, the occasion depending on the nature and substance of your problem or concern. This technique of imagining what your selected mental advisors would say, do, or recommend, has worked for others far more wealthy and influential than I am. It has also worked for me. Why not for you? Though the race track of time has ruts in the fairest of faces, successful achievers never retire from self-improvement and the uniting of character with intellect.

The next primary step in the development of a pleasant personality is to extend more of yourself to the world around you. Pay attention to your manner of dress. Since most of us dress to please others, this observation must tell you something. Where can you find the courage to speak forcefully in front of others? How can you become a more agreeable person? Late in life you may be fatigued from years of work and your efforts to raise a family. What changes in yourself must you make to control your anger and frustrations? You may feel that people do not appreciate you; and you're at risk of being misunderstood for practicing your faith. Jesus said to his disciples that many would be hated and persecuted because they were not of this world.

Begin looking for the good qualities in those you meet and associate with. Compliments, when given as an outgrowth of this habit, will be genuine, since they come from the heart. This is not some "quickie" habit that can be acquired overnight. Your loves, unlike your tastes, are not meant to change with your fortunes. If at dusk you lived from hand to mouth, lacked general confidence, and possessed a somber personality, you could not, at the dawning of a new day, obtain credibility by raising a crop of sudden compliments and driving a shiny new Cadillac. Your behavior would be suspect. You may not be, now, what you used to be; but change, nevertheless, must come from the heart, and this process develops gradually. If too many of your thoughts are directed inward (because of ego), you will turn people off and lose your ability to influence them. Think about this definition of personality: What a person has when they make you feel the same way about them as you do about yourself.

SCRIPT AND FLAME

Dale Carnegie, whose book on personality development, *How to Win Friends and Influence People*, which is one of the all-time best sellers, stresses that the way to a new and vibrant personality lies, first, within the mind of the individual. You must be able to influence your own mind by developing a positive mental attitude before you can influence others in any way. We discussed the fear of progressive age earlier in this book. Of course, the unwelcome shadow of Alzheimer's disease can lurk behind us as we trod down the bewildering path of aging. Nevertheless, we must exercise our minds as well as our bodies. A clear mind, the search for memories, and active control over our thoughts, are worthwhile pursuits. The constant strive for self-improvement and intellectual challenges, such as reading, writing, painting, music, employment, walking, and hobbies, are critical exercises for our minds no matter how much our physical bodies are weakened by age.

Carnegie says in his book: ***"All I desire is dominion over myself; dominion over my thoughts; dominion over my fears; dominion over my mind and over my spirit. And the wonderful thing is that I know I can attain this dominion to an astonishing degree, any time I want to, by merely controlling my actions, which, in turn, control my reactions."*** You may ask how to control temptations involving lustful sex, food, revenge, hate, etc. The answer is to block such thoughts and change the channel of your mind to other subjects, lest the reflections, like demons, will continue to run wild in your memory. **Essentially, your life is given form by your thoughts.**

"Serene I fold my hands and wait, nor care for wind, nor tide, nor sea; I rave no more 'gainst time or fate, for lo, my own shall come to me."

– **Burroughs**

Referring back to **SUCCESS RULE #3** on Self-confidence, we see the importance of the subconscious mind in altering behavior characteristics. Remember that you begin to influence the subconscious mind through the process of autosuggestion (self-hypnosis). This process is largely oral—you must habitually repeat aloud those goals and behavior characteristics you expect to reach and adopt. In the case of character development (the foundation of a pleasant personality) you make it a habit of becoming more like those you admire (your invisible cabinet of advisors). **Aristotle said that a good character carries with it the highest power of causing a thing to be believed.** First you must believe that you are developing a more pleasant personality through cultivation of the proper habits. Here, in summary, are the proper habits for us to develop for the creation of new brain cells. Mental qualities you learn and practice in this life are carried in your eternal soul.

SCRIPT AND FLAME

1. Repeat to yourself that you are adopting those qualities of character and behavior patterns you find admirable in your imaginary cabinet. Many followers of Christ have achieved the dominant part of their character and behavior objectives through worship and prayer. Perform or pray this ritual daily until it becomes a habit.

2. Find opportunities to speak forcefully to others on topics of interest to them. Avoid controversy at this time.

3. Learn to control your nervous system and to become more agreeable. Avoid expressing your grievances and anger in front of others. *(Free speech recess is given here for emotional outbursts and expressions emanating from political and sports activities and protests against perceived unjust laws, regulations and legal rulings.)*

4. Remember the importance of your outward appearance. Your dress, as well as your behavior, is your table of contents.

5. Form the habit of making compliments from the heart.

6. Stick to your resolutions. Clear away half-finished tasks.

7. Devote your wholehearted effort to developing a positive attitude.

8. Remember that a personality change cannot be brought about overnight. Begin with small things, and build from there.

9. Recognize that because of the following inviolable rule, a pleasant personality can only come about through practice: ***Use breeds habit, and habit is stronger than nature.***

10. Don't be discouraged by occasional failures in your efforts to improve yourself. The expectations of life depend upon diligence; the mechanic who would perfect his work must first sharpen his tools.

11. Improve your memory with exercise. Studies have shown that physically able people who began to exercise in their 60's have reduced their risk of dementia by half.

12. Take up a new hobby such as music, painting, or foreign languages.

MONEY LESSON LEARNED: Trust not your money with schemers and trickster personalities. Look for good character as a standard in all with whom you do business.

Chapter 12
SCRIP(T) and FLAME RULE #10
Practice <u>TOLERANCE</u> and Patience

What do you see when you look into the eyes of a newborn child? Wickedness? Spitefulness? Cruelty? Of course not. If such characteristics were inherited, you would see signs, much like the striving of a snake to bite, or a tiny tiger to tear and claw at you. All children come into this world with nothing but innocence, gentleness, and fear. They are about as limited in their instinct toward mischief and destruction as pigeons and rabbits. Mankind's emotional tendencies, such as tolerance, grow mainly from our social heredity; these instincts are largely rooted in our physical heredity. I make this point about children to emphasize that, because intolerance is acquired, it can, with determined effort, be "unlearned."

Tolerance, it is said, is the only real test of civilization, exemplified in the lives of great leaders such as presidents Lincoln, F.D. Roosevelt and Eisenhower, who all reached across party lines with forgiveness to their political adversaries in the most difficult times of our nation. We can even find similar forbearance in much maligned President Trump, the "Gladiator," who opened the iron curtain between his enemies, seriously considering some for his cabinet, while exchanging his towering castle in New York City for a humble white cabin in the swamps of D.C.

The principle of tolerance is essential to aging and success because without it you will ultimately lose the game of life—fallible beings always fail somewhere. If you can "unlearn" the tendencies to hate, to spite, and to persecute those whose views are different from your own; if you can look dispassionately at those you disagree with, you are likely to find their motives to be more pure than you thought and their judgments less biased than your mind would lead you to believe.

It is known that our brains shrink with the ripening of age. Neurochemical and physiological transmittals are slower; and you'll probably find that your adversary's reasoning is based on the same data as yours, though he or she may have arrived at a different conclusion.

SCRIPT AND FLAME

A wise observer of man's emotional tendencies once said, "Give me the control of the child until it is twelve years old, and you can teach the child any religion you may please after that time, for I will have planted my own religion so deeply in the child's mind that no power on earth could undo my work." Hitler knew this. Here was one of the most intolerant men who ever walked the face of the earth; and he perpetrated his intolerance through the Hitler Youth movement. If he had been able to hold tight to these youths for a single generation, he could have forced his warped ideas upon their minds so effectively that they could not have resisted the brain washing efforts. However, no power on earth can force impenetrable entrenchments in the human mind; and those poor souls now suffering in mental slavery under dictators and tyrants will—at some point in their eternal soul— reject militarized mind control and embrace God's gift to his children of free thought and speech. Jesus gained the attention and support of the world through the strength and transfer of thoughts.

Of all our delusions, none is perhaps greater than the thought that our past has ruined our present, that the evils we have done, the mistakes we have made, the misdeeds we have committed, have made swamps of our hopes. Remember, that as we grow up, we no longer act and speak like children; and we are always older than we were. Evils of yesteryear are gone with the wind; so we can always act to restore balance to our thought process.

In some of the world's emerging nations, you can still see perpetuation of *intolerance* through ruthless leaders who, like Hitler, have gained control of the schools and the media, while subverting organized religion. Since schools, media, and religion are the three main avenues through which social heredity operates, it is easy to see how such unfit traits as *intolerance* can be nurtured and kept alive in the name of nationalism, religious extremism, or caliphates. Cognitive decline, as we age, allows the weeds of *intolerance* to grow and spread in our thought process. William Penn said, "It would be better to be of no church than to be bitter for any."

Two men were having a conversation on the street, and one grew worried over the other's *intolerant* attitude toward Jews. "Isn't that just like a Jew?" the bigot said. When the question was raised again, the more tolerant man replied as follows:

"Which Jew do you mean, Shylock or Christ?" The point was clearly made, and the bigot must have understood that such flagrant generalities about whole classes of people are open to questions by those of wiser vision. The next time somebody says to you, "Isn't that just like a Black?" You can reply by asking, "Which Black do you mean, Uncle Tom, Jackie Robinson, or Martin Luther King?"

Children, as a class of mankind, seem always to be serving on the front line of impatience. If you would improve your patience level, it certainly will help you to begin with children. Jesus said, "Of such is the kingdom of Heaven." Most of us are inclined to say, "You kids are making too much noise." The next time it occurs to you to comment harshly on the noise level, remember your urge to raise your patience level. The time may have already come too soon, when beside your rocking chair, you'd give the world to hear the ringing laughter that once disturbed you.

In Dale Carnegie's perennial best-seller, *How to Win Friends and Influence People*, is reprinted this stirring essay on patience. The author is a Hall of Fame tennis player from the turn of the 20th century era:

FATHER FORGETS - by W. Livingston Larned

Listen, son: I am saying this to you as you lie asleep, one little paw crumpled under your cheek and the blond curls stickily wet on your damp forehead. I have stolen into your room alone, just a few minutes ago. As I sat reading my paper, a stifling wave of remorse swept over me. Guiltily, I came to your bedside.

These are the things I was thinking, son: I had been cross to you. I scolded you as you were dressing for school because you gave your face merely a dab with a towel. I took you to task for not cleaning your shoes. I called out angrily when you threw some of your things on the floor. At breakfast I found fault, too. You spilled things. You gulped down your food. You put your elbows on the table. You spread butter too thick on

your bread. And as you started off to play, and I made my train, you turned and waved a hand and called, "Goodbye, Daddy" and I frowned and said in reply, "Hold your shoulders back!"

Then it began all over in the late afternoon. As I came up the road I spied you, down on your knees, playing marbles. There were holes in your stockings. I humiliated you before your boy friends by marching you ahead of me into the house. Stockings were expensive—and if you had to buy them you would be more careful. Do you remember, later, when I was reading in the library, how you came in, timidly, with a sort of hurt look in your eyes? When I glanced up over my paper, impatient with the interruption, you hesitated at the door. "What is it you want?" I snapped.

You said nothing, but ran across in one tempestuous plunge, and threw your arms around my neck and kissed me; and your small arms tightened with an affection that God had set blooming in your heart and which neglect could not wither. And then you were gone, pattering up the stairs. Well, son, it was shortly afterward that my paper slipped from my hands and a terrible sickening fear came over me. What has habit been doing to me? The habit of finding fault, of reprimanding—this was my reward for you being a boy. It was not that I didn't love you; it was just that I expected too much of youth. I was measuring you by the yardstick of my own years.

And there was so much that was good and fine and true in your character. The little heart in you was as big as the dawn itself over the wide hills. This was shown by your spontaneous impulse to rush in and kiss me goodnight. Nothing else matters tonight, son. I have come to your bedside in the darkness; and I have dwelt there, ashamed!

It is a feeble atonement; I know you would not understand these things if I told them to you during your waking hours. But tomorrow I will be a real Daddy! I will play with you, and suffer when you suffer, and laugh when you laugh. I will bite my tongue when impatient words come. I will keep saying as if it were a ritual: He is nothing but a boy–a little boy! I am afraid I have visualized you as a man. Yet I see you now, son, crumpled and weary in your cot; I see that you are still a baby. Yesterday you were in your mother's arms, your head on her shoulder. I have asked too much, too much.

Whenever you come into contact with people, remember this essay on impatience. Your situation in life may be very demanding and frustrating, leaving little time toward others for consideration and simple courtesies. Who will remind you that your patience level is receding? Perhaps there will be no little boy to spring forward with his arms full of love for you, despite your failings.

Like the other success principles discussed in this chapter, you must work at mastering or regaining the art of *patience* and *tolerance*, or risk shivering off into a lonely life of self-pity. Become a model to yourself, rather than a critic of others. Not only do children need someone to look up to, so do most people react favorably to those with *patience* and tolerance; and it is only through the cooperation of others that you can achieve true and lasting success as a person. With *patience*, everything comes in due season, whether in childhood, adulthood, or in the shadow of life.

It is worth remembering that the noiseless foot of time often brings forth childhood characteristics in people, such as falling down, putting names to faces, and unsteady memory of things to do—all the more easy reasons why folks should be patient and tolerant with elders, many of whom suffer from hearing loss affecting encoding information in the brain.

MONEY LESSON LEARNED: Money that comes quickly goes quickly away. Take care of your money as you would your time.

Chapter 13
SCRIPT AND (F)LAME RULE #11
Learn to Profit from FAILURE

"Of all the sad words of tongue and pen, the saddest are these: It might have been." – Whittier

There is no more anguished plea on earth than the lament from the person who wishes their time spent revoked, that they might try again to accomplish what they might have done, to find happiness they might have found, and to be the person they might have been. They never hurtled life's great obstacles because life's smaller obstacles held them back. If they view themselves as a failure—and most people count their misgivings—it is not that the breaks were against them, but only that their determinations to succeed were not strong enough. A succession of temporary defeats—if you fail to learn from them—can often be counted as failures. And the only person who never fails at anything is the person who never does anything. We all succeed in life by trying not to make the same mistakes over and over again. Failure is not an undertaker—it is a teacher; it is not defeat—it is delay; it is not a dead-end street—it is a temporary detour. **Consider the slippery nature of my youth**:

"It was dark, and I was alone, except for my puppy. There was no electricity or coal heat in the deserted shanty; but my disrupted family had left behind an old wind-up phonograph. I played the record, *Red River Valley*, and drifted off to sleep. When I woke up, I packed a few belongings in my bicycle basket, along with my puppy, and peddled off to the city from an unhappy home. After an exhaustive search, I somehow found the restaurant where my mother worked as a waitress. My childhood gone, I finally settled into a crowded back room of uprooted and confused siblings."

"My next stop was to find a job, the nearest thing to a home. In the morning, I woke up—a 15-year-old kid and high school dropout—still alone on my path in life, and with no discernable hope, and with nowhere to turn. In my mind, we were poor, and this was the way things worked in the world; but I never felt defeated. I just kept on moving."

SCRIPT AND FLAME

> ➢ OBSTACLES EXIST NOT TO STOP YOU, BUT TO GO OVER THEM.
>
> ➢ A LOSS IS NOT A SETBACK, BUT AN OPPORTUNITY TO ATTACK.

In my office I have a framed sign that reads:

NEVER ADMIT DEFEAT

Failed in business	('31)
Defeated for legislature	('32)
Again failed in business	('33)
Elected to legislature	('34)
Sweetheart died	('35)
Had nervous breakdown	('36)
Defeated for Speaker	('38)
Defeated for Elector	('40)
Elected to Congress	('46)
Son died	('50)
Defeated for Senate	('55)
Defeated for Vice President	('56)
Defeated for Senate	('58)
Elected President	('60)

Just a few rough spots in the life of Abraham Lincoln – a failure in his destiny until age 51. **He said: "Always bear in mind that your own resolution to succeed is more important than any other."**

On August 17, 1978, French villagers looked up from the tiny hamlet of Miserey and watched the helium-filled balloon, Double Eagle II, float closer to its landing in Normandy. "Vive les Americains!" went the shout from the ground. Hats were tossed in the air. People abandoned their cars along the country road and sprinted toward a nearby grain field. History was in the making.

Soon three Americans named Anderson, Newman, and Ambruzzo were drinking champagne atop the shoulders of ecstatic Frenchmen who shouted, "Formidable! Formidable!" Other Frenchmen scrambled to the scene and began tearing "souvenirs" from the first manned balloon to cross the Atlantic Ocean. The crossing was risky. An earlier attempt had nearly cost the Americans' lives as they plunged into the freezing waters off of Iceland. Seventeen earlier expeditions had failed, and five men had died in pursuit of this elusive dream. Failure gnawed relentlessly at the men aboard Eagle II. At first, their radio system went out, forcing them to rely on a crude ham radio. Then, over the mid-Atlantic, the ice buildup on top of the balloon was so heavy that the balloonists lost nearly 3,000 feet in altitude. Sandbags, lead, potatoes—all precious ballast—were tossed overboard in a desperate attempt to stabilize the craft. Nearing the Irish coastline, the balloon plunged 2,000 feet in a perilous brush with the sea.

The men knew that if more ballast were dropped over the side they would probably not reach Ireland; but past failures had turned out to be blessings, because they taught the balloonists such needed lessons of perseverance, courage, self-discipline, and a well-defined power of decision. They continued to endure until the sun had warmed the balloon and caused it to rise again. Finally, the wind nearly abandoned the team altogether. They quickly discarded the remainder of the ballast. As fast as the ax tore into the floorboards of the gondola, weighty timber was tossed over the side, along with cables, radio equipment, and heavy clothing.

In great attempts, it is glorious even to fail; but it was doubtful that this truth could have been believed at the time. As people never thoroughly understand truth until they have challenged it; so do they shun familiarity with failure until they have suffered from one and seen themselves triumph where others have failed. When the balloonists landed in France, the great truth about failure was brought home to them. <u>Every failure carries with it the seed of an equivalent benefit</u>. Past defeats had been a blessing to the team, for they were signaled to move at another time and place; and they acted upon that signal as if it were a detour sign and not a dead-end street.

Ralph Waldo Emerson, in his great essay of compensation, wrote of the duality that underlies the nature and condition of man.

"Every excess causes a defect; every defect an excess. Every sweet hath its sour; every evil its good. Every faculty which is a receiver of pleasure, has an equal penalty put on its abuse. It is to answer for its moderation with its life. For every grain of wit there is a grain of folly. For everything you have missed, you have gained something else; and for everything you gain, you lose something. If riches increase, they are increased that use them. If the gatherer gathers too much, nature takes out of the man what she puts in his chest, swells the estate, but kills the owner. Nature hates monopolies and exceptions. . . . There is always some leveling circumstance that puts down the overbearing, the strong, the rich, the fortunate, substantially on the same ground."

<u>For every failure there is a triumph</u>. In real life, as in fiction, the human animal is most courageous, most interesting, most respected and admired, when snatching victory from the jaws of defeat. Remember, too, that it is contrary to nature's laws to accept failure without seeking a corresponding benefit. To blame defeat on "bad luck" is to accuse nature of abridging her own laws, and this she

never does. An example is the controversial election of 2016 where the political tables were turned by natural forces in the electorate seeking long overdue corrections in government policies and power structure.

For the faithful among us, Fr. Joseph Esper, in his book, *Saintly Solutions*, explains how the most saintly Biblical figures were faced down with failures. Apostle Peter once said to Jesus, "Depart from me, for I am a sinful man, Oh Lord." This holder of the "golden keys" and a man who had the life of Jesus in his hands, was at one time a proud, boastful, impetuous, and cowardly figure, who first slept through the forceful seizure of his Master, then ran away in fear, denying that he ever knew Christ, leaving the Savior to be beaten, tortured and nailed on a rugged cross to die for our sins. All of these human failings were failures of the flesh; however divine grace was promised by the Lord to repentant believers.

And remember, many saints and popes throughout history were known to have been failures in other degrees of their lives. Jesus, the unequaled Lord of Learning who upraised mankind, taught us that just over the hills of our sins lies hope that we will be judged by our faithfulness and not by our failures in life.

To ensure yourself from failure, you must understand the laws of the universe and adapt yourself to their habits. The words, "I can't" are, after all, merely a statement of opinion and not a fact. Nature and behavioral sages tell us that anything the mind can conceive and believe, can be achieved. Your only limitations are those which you set up in your mind or allow others to establish for you. If you accept an experience as a failure, such as financial or family difficulties, broken friendships, or false accusations about you, then you will have failed. But you will have failed in your mind alone!

Never accept an experience as a failure, because your mind will then direct your actions toward defeat. Classify your set-backs as delays, detours, and educational experiences. Your mind will then act accordingly to extract the ultimate triumph. It matters little what others may call your experiences, because they are yours alone—be it related to gossip, marital problems, habitual criticism, or whatever. You can classify them any way you choose. Yours is the only verdict that counts. To break yourself of the habit of failure, you must first identify the root causes. You'll want to coax them out of hiding and destroy them one by one. Habits, once formed, are not easily broken; but the battle is already half won when you identify the basic causes.

A list of fifty MAJOR FAILURE HABITS follows. How many can you spot within yourself?

1. Lack of chief goals in life
2. Lack of self-confidence
3. Inability to take control of your own mind

4. Succumbing to any or all of the 7 basic fears
5. Accepting mediocrity as a standard
6. Procrastination
7. Lack of persistent endeavor
8. Lack of a positive mental attitude
9. Sour personality
10. Lack of gratitude for life's blessings
11. Expecting something for nothing
12. Inability to make decisions
13. Lack of personal knowledge and experience
14. Over-emphasis on formal learning
15. Unwillingness to take chances
16. Impatient attitude
17. Inability to accurately judge people
18. Lack of cooperative attitude
19. Over-emphasis on material concerns
20. Loss of harmony in marriage
21. Loss of spirituality
22. Inability to cultivate true friendships
23. Selfishness and greed
24. Uncontrolled envy
25. Lack of work effort

26. Indiscriminate spending

27. Dishonesty

28. Inaccurate thinking

29. Excessive ego

30. Lack of savings and capital

31. Intolerance

32. Abuse of power

33. Lack of enthusiasm

34. Lack of labor of love

35. Jack-of-all-trades syndrome

36. Excessive superstition and prejudice

37. Inability to discipline yourself

38. Lack of loyalty

39. Uncontrolled emotions

40. Lack of imagination

41. Inability to recognize opportunity

42. Unwillingness to do more than you're paid for

43. Vindictive attitude

44. Minding other peoples' business

45. Using vulgarity and slander

46. Lack of respect for constitutional authority

47. Unwillingness to accept advice and counsel

> **48. Carelessness in settling obligations to others**
>
> **49. Drug use and alcoholism**
>
> **50. Unjustified trust in people**

Pick out the failure habits that you feel have held you back. Write them down on a card or slip of paper and tell yourself (orally) at least twice a day that you are overcoming all undesirable habits. Your brain will do the rest as you see the habits fade away. You want your subconscious mind to believe that you will not tolerate any of the "fatal fifty" failure habits.

Remember that you reach the subconscious mind (which controls your actions) through the technique of *autosuggestion,* or self-hypnosis. **If you repeat a statement to yourself long enough, you will begin to believe it, whether it is true or not.** This is so because the thought will be imbedded in your subconscious mind; hence it reflects itself through your actions and attitudes. You can develop, at will, the inspiration to overcome bad habits; and once that inspiration is transformed into action you have the most important ingredient to succeed known to man.

This self-help activity will help your brain to grow so it can store and retrieve information more easily. An unused mind tends to lose power and opens itself up to cognitive decline. Remember that this mind exercise can only work for you if you use the technique on a regular basis.

Shakespeare was one of the greatest observers of mankind's habits, actions and tendencies the world has ever known.

When the immortal bard says, "Assume a virtue if you have it not," he is suggesting that we look the part, dress the part, and act the part of being successful and in control of our lifestyle, so we can skip feelings of failure. To become successful and happy in life, you must first convince your subconscious mind that success in your lifestyle and happiness are what you want. Here is a self-help quiz to see if you can banish feelings of failure from your life:

1. **Do you know what you want out of your future life?**
2. **Do you want it badly enough?**
3. **Do you confidently expect to achieve your goals?**
4. **Are you persistently determined to reach your goals?**
5. **Are you willing to pay the price for achieving them, even if it means reaching out to others for assistance?**

Obviously this quiz calls for affirmative answers. If we cannot answer "yes" to all of the questions, we can see ourselves bogged down in life. Shakespeare described the process of an uncertain and aimless life on earth:

And so, from hour to hour, we ripe and ripe, and then from hour to hour we will rot and rot.

Don't, however, be so recklessly bent on success that you press on without sound judgment and consideration for others. When you set a task for yourself, it is a good habit to complete the task; therefore, do not harbor desires that are too many, too confusing, and beyond your training or ability to accomplish. Difficult and impractical tasks can often cost you harmony in your business or relationships. People around you can sense when your ego or aspirations have gotten out of hand. Remember this: An honest effort to understand your abilities and determination, and to make improvements within yourself is not the same as amassing folly and ego.

John Paul Getty, the billionaire philanthropist died at 84. He compared the process of achieving success in life with an experience in a fine restaurant. In his book, *The Golden Age*, he wrote:

1. Don't expect to find every dish you want on the menu.
2. You can, however, find enough variety to satisfy hunger and palate.
3. While eating, never bite off more than you can chew.

4. Take healthful amounts; any food worth taking is not to be toyed with.

Like gluttonous and unhealthy eating habits, boorishness in one's social relationships is generally rooted in a fear of certain inadequacies. Failure habits are aggravated if you talk more than you listen. Not only do you fail to gain useful knowledge, but you also disclose your plans and objectives to potential enemies who, through envy, may wish to see you cut down a notch or two. Defeating the habits of failure is best accomplished with deeds, not empty words.

MONEY LESSON LEARNED: If you desire to help others with your money, make sure you will not bring unnecessary burdens on yourself.

Chapter 14
SCRIPT and F(L)AME RULE #12
Learn to LEAD and Harmonize with Others

The greatest fortune of an army, or a people, is to keep ignorant persons from leadership and secure the wisest men to win the battles.

Someone asked a famous conductor of a great symphony orchestra which orchestral instrument he considered the most difficult to play. The conductor thought a moment; then answered: "Second fiddle. I can get plenty of first violinists; but to find one who can play second fiddle with enthusiasm—that's a problem. And if we have no second fiddles, we have no harmony!"

This story points up the necessity for learning to work with and for others before you can expect to lead and harmonize with them. And, as pointed out earlier in this book, the way to wealth and independence in your own life is measured by your ability to influence others. The ability to "make friends and influence people" is largely an acquired habit—leaders are made, not born. And it is said that one old person who has carried his heart in his hand, like a palm branch, waving all discords into peace—leads us to faith in God, in ourselves, and in each other, more than many sermons. Proper training in the military can make a *dumbhead* into a leader in eight weeks; but building character is a life-long task.

In Edgar Puryear's excellent study of leadership, *Nineteen Stars*, the author emphasizes that the great generals of World War II, Marshall, MacArthur, Eisenhower, Patton, and Rommel spent their entire military careers preparing for high command through study, and through working as junior officers for the most outstanding generals. Leadership (and initiative) is but one of the sixteen essential qualities to success in life and, not surprisingly, the best leaders are those who have mastered all sixteen qualities. In the military, however, effective leadership is often a matter of life and death; and its importance is not to be minimized. Marine General James "Mad Dog" Mattis, said this of the Iraqi Republican Guard in 2003: "Either the Commander of the Fifty-first Mechanized Division is going to surrender to me, or his guys are going to die." History reveals that gentleness—which is not to kill or be killed to destroy the evil that assaults life—is not benign. It is weakness. Many living leaders are only mediocre; and many dead ones are myths.

SCRIPT AND FLAME

The principles of leadership apply as much to the person of any age who aspires to a level of success in civilian life as they do to future generals. The principles are standard rules for both. And think of 74-year-old Senator Bernie Sanders in 2016—an ex-hippie, running for President of the United States, chalking up millions of dollars in small change contributions, while influencing record numbers of young supporters to follow him. **Age is a matter of feelings, not of years.**

For purposes of this discussion, we will assume that *leadership* and *initiative* go hand in hand. You must, first, know yourself, your job or situation in life—how to get yourself going in the morning—before you can understand others and expect to motivate them. This wisdom is contained in an old adage about *leadership: Know your people; know your business; know yourself.*

Before examining a definitive list of known and proven *leadership* qualities, it will be useful for you to assess and evaluate your own initiative. The world will, indeed, make way for, and follow, the person who knows where he or she is going and how to get there.

This characteristic is self-evident in the life of President Harry S. Truman, who was able to beat all imaginary odds to hold onto the presidency, while trading *his degree of intemperance for the mantle of statesman of* the greatest country on earth.

Pledge to yourself that you will soon be able to answer *yes* to the following questions:

1. Do you have a chief goal in life; and are you adopting the proper habits that will make your goal a reality?

2. Are you whipping the habit of procrastination?

3. Are you acquiring the habit of doing more than is expected of you?

As you can see from the prior questions, initiative is basically a habit that can be built into yourself through conscious effort. If you're short on initiative in the big things of life, then begin by improving yourself at home and on the job. Memorize and begin to practice the success principles in this book that are based on the code words – SCRIPT and FLAME. Accomplish one small task each day that you've been putting off. Find things to do in your daily work or routine for which you do not expect monetary compensation. Small habits seem to gather by unseen degrees, and eventually they form larger habits, much as brooks and streams make rivers, which in turn run down to the sea. As the result of practicing initiative, you'll find yourself attracting the attention of those who will place greater value on your services. Initiative, then, is the gateway to opportunity and *leadership*. And, understandably, initiative opens the door to life's great riches. Oddly enough, these riches are not based on wealth, but reflect on you as a person. They are hidden in your heart and mind.

Great leaders, as a rule, have multitudes of followers; and this is true because people hope to gain in some way through their association or affiliation with the great and successful. Since you are reading this book for purposes of self-improvement and independence from the hardships and difficulties in life, the reader is encouraged to understand more about the attitudes and *leadership* qualities of those who have built great fortunes, this to reinforce the fact that a singular pursuit of amassing riches does not go hand to hand with the goal of obtaining enduring happiness and contentment. F. Scott Fitzgerald is reported to have once remarked to Ernest Hemmingway, "You know, the rich are different from you and me." To which Hemmingway replied, "I know, they have more money."

God examines both rich and poor, not according to their lands and houses, but according to the riches of their hearts. - *Augustine*

THE PARADOX OF RICHES

Those who have made and perpetuated great wealth without loss of peace of mind, all understand that the virtue of money is in its use, not in its quantity. Carnegie, Rockefeller, and Ford, all came to realize this and gave away millions to charitable causes before they died. Elvis Presley, seeking answers to his fame and fortune, and interpreting his twin brother's death at birth as a message from God, sought answers to the mystery of life by such foolish capers as giving away brand new Cadillac cars to the poor and friends, and tossing money around like candy, then seeking eternal youth in his bathroom while searching for the Son of God in a drug overdose. The Beatles, awash in money, and assuming they were of more interest to the world than Christ, searched for inner peace through participation in psychic rituals, kneeling to spiritual guides from India, and venturing out in the world on weird metaphysical pursuits.

All that live must die, passing through nature to eternity– *Shakespeare*

Bill Gates and Warren Buffett, edged on by destiny and their over-proportioned lives on earth, pledged half of their fortunes to charity; and Steve Jobs, an idealistic and stoic Silicon Valley multi-billionaire, generated an army of young techie millionaires and was summoned up yonder, a generation before his retirement years, by the ultimate monarch.

It is true in many cases that the person without money is at the mercy of the person who has it. And the fact prevails that people will weigh you largely in the light of your bank account or credit rating—no matter who you are, your age, or what you are capable of accomplishing. The penalty of *leadership*, nevertheless, is often envy, hate, and suspicion from smaller minds. Great leaders, as a rule, have learned to practice the positive emotions; and they have no time to waste with a desire to malign or injure others. If they did these wrongs, they would not be great leaders.

SUCCESS MAKES SUCCESS IN AGING AS SUCCESS HELPS TO GROW RICH

As we grow old, we tend to grow more foolish but also wiser. People will rapidly, willingly, and voluntarily follow the person who shows initiative.

They will not, however, willingly follow the schemer who is after their money and who is motivated primarily toward seeking material gain. Successful aging calls for an awareness of the following rewards:

LIFE'S TRUE REWARDS FOR SUCCESSFUL AGING

1. Freedom from fear
2. Love of one's work
3. Harmony with others
4. Definite future plans
5. Good health
6. Economic security
7. Sharing with others
8. Control of self
9. Hope for the future
10. Positive attitude toward life
11. Open mind
12. Concern for others

You will notice that all of these rewards are repeated in the list of known and proven leadership qualities. Remember, now, that effective leadership is *one* of the fundamental principles you need to acquire for the achievement of personal success. Be honest, and rate yourself as being either, *good, fair,* or *poor* in each of the qualities. When you have mastered the principles of effective *leadership*, along with the other 15 success principles, you will possess the finest insurance policy against failure known to mankind—whether you are primarily seeking material gains or simply peace of mind.

EFFECTIVE LEADERSHIP QUALITIES

In politics, it is curious that we often follow alleged leaders for what they say, not for what they do—one persona for show and another side for a secret life behind the scenes.

The providence of devoted followers in the long run is shaped by those who adopt the inner side of the leader. You will note in the qualities below, the dominance of all of the 16 RULES forming the basis of this book.

1. Freedom from fear
2. Control of self
3. Concern for others
4. Selflessness
5. Ability to delegate
6. Sense of justice
7. Accurate thought patterns
8. Tolerance and Patience
9. Temperance
10. Integrity
11. Ability to profit from failure
12. Courage to make decisions
13. Doing more than required

14. Attention to detail

15. Imaginative outlook

16. Humility

17. Willingness to be responsible

18. Team builder

19. Tactful personality

20. Concentration, persistence

21. Practice of the Golden Rule

22. Taking the initiative

23. Acting with enthusiasm

24. Cooperate with others

25. Willingness to work, prepare

26. Definite goals and plans

27. Confidence in self

28. Ability to follow through

29. Dedication to duty

30. Respect for authority

31. Showmanship

MONEY LESSON LEARNED: Lead not yourself into the pit of hopeless debt where you may struggle vainly for years.

Chapter 15
SCRIPT and FL(A)ME RULE #13
Have a Definite Chief AIM in Life

After graduating from college, I married and wandered for a number of years in search of myself, hoping to find out what I wanted to do in life. I considered law, went to grad school, dropped out; and, along the line, I tried song writing, acting, vending, ad writing, sales, horse livery, and real estate. You could easily have described me as a rudderless young man with more than his quota of frustration, melancholy, and fear—all elements for which the cure would be a *definite* labor of love or a *chief goal* in life. Years later, when I began to set down goals for myself in real estate, I found success creeping up on me like the tide. *Specific desire,* of course, was my ship of fortune; while *specific goals* were my charts through the rough seas of life.

Let's review for a moment how concentrated thought on specifics can literally part the storm waters of life and open up the channels to a successful life. Concentrated thought is aimed at reaching and influencing the subconscious mind into action. Ralph Waldo Emerson reduced the process into a single sentence: *"As a man thinketh, so is he, and as a man chooseth, so is he."* Mere wishing and vague goal-setting won't work for you, since these *longings and aspirations* do not penetrate the depths of the mind. To successfully continue your journey through life, you must either restore or conceive a grand purpose and form a deep subconscious belief in reaching your goal(s); only then can your belief become the foundation of reality.

All of us, in our journey on the sea of life, will eventually be patching up our bodies for Heaven, because life is not only to live, but to live well. However the specter of illness, loss, tragedy and stress appears to loom larger in our lives as we age. In her book, *Successful Aging,* author Mary O'Brian, M.D. exposes common myths about older individuals and their degree of productiveness. She writes that it would take three million paid full-time workers to provide the same level of assistance to others in need, as is now provided by seniors. Even at advanced old age, an overwhelming majority of seniors show comparatively few signs of functional disability; and only about 5% live in nursing homes. So those who have a measure of good health and attitude, energy, and physical ability have hope for the future; and hope is everything.

For those of any age in whom hope springs eternal, and who are blessed with the crutch of time, here is an amplification of the proven step-by-step procedure for reaching and influencing the subconscious mind. (RULE #4)

1. Write out a statement of your desires, such as a specific amount of money you will need to reach your level of comfort.

2. Determine in your statement exactly what services you intend to render in return for the money, such as vigorous and unremitting effort in some field of endeavor for your age and physical condition.

3. Establish a *definite* time frame and a specific date in your statement.

4. *Conceive* a workable plan for carrying out your desire, and *believe* you will soon achieve your goal(s) by implementing the plan whether it is completely ready or not. Express this belief in your statement.

5. Express *gratitude* in your statement for having been given the guidance necessary to carry out your plan.

6. Proceed with *enthusiasm,* and do not be dissuaded in your efforts to reach your goal. Affirm this in your statement.

7. Anticipate accomplishment of your goal by repeating in your statement that you will soon be in possession of the *specified* desires.

8. Read your written statement aloud—at least once in the morning and again at night—and, while reading, *see, feel*, and *believe* yourself in possession of your desires.

One of life's great truths is the axiom that <u>general desires are but weak longings</u>; and that they have the habit of leading you onward to failure after failure. When you set *definite chief* goals for yourself and come to terms with *exactly* what you want from life, you'll discover your labor of love and find the ways to reach your goals. Remember the following:

Achievement of your definite aim and goals in life is dependent upon the degree of force, energy, will, determination and persistence with which you pursue your objectives. You can have or be anything you want—if you only want it hard enough.

Napoleon Hill spent fourteen years analyzing more than 16,000 men and women for his *Laws of Success* course. He discovered that 95% of these people had to struggle, almost unbearably, to find happiness and the ordinary necessities in life. In other words, those with wandering minds could be classified as failures. Here's what Dr. Hill says of the test group:

One of the most startling facts brought to light by those 16,000 analyses was the discovery that the ninety-five percent who were classed as failures were in that class because they had no *definite chief aim* in life, while the five percent constituting the successful participants not only had purposes that were *definite,* but they also had *definite* plans for the attainment of their goals in life. The following psychological attitudes are mindful to dramatize and characterize human approaches toward the search for happiness in life—*hedonism* and *Eudaimonia. Hedonism* refers to over-indulgence in the search for happiness and pleasure in life, as in a fat kitchen or the pursuit of lavish sex; while *Eudaimonia* is about a life of activity governed by reason—as in true love or the sight of a sane and sober man on horseback. A study at the University of Rochester reported that graduates with positive thoughts and specified objectives in life far outshined—both physically and mentally—their classmates who followed a lifestyle beseeched with carefree thoughts and extrinsic objectives. Philosophically, it would appear from this study that contentment in life is a form of un-repented pleasure, and that true wisdom is the price of real happiness.

Preceding accomplishment in any field of endeavor (your chief aim) must be *desire*; and desires must be strong and *definite* if they are to be achieved. Every great accomplishment of any man or woman at any time first had to exist as a *thought* before it could exist; and grand desires proceed from grand thoughts. Consider this time-worn passage from a wise writer, Robert Collier, in his book. *The Secret of the Ages:*

"Every deed that we do, good or bad, is prompted by DESIRE. We are charitable because we wish to relieve our inner stress at the sight of suffering; or from the urge of

sympathy, with its desire to express its nature; or from the desire to be respected in this world; or to secure a comfortable place in the next one.

"*One man is kind because he desires to be kind—because it gives him satisfaction and content to be so. One man does his duty because he desires to do it. He obtains a higher emotional satisfaction and content from duty well done than he would from neglecting his duty in accordance with some opposing desires. Another man yields to the desire to shirk his duty. He obtains greater satisfaction and content from refraining from performing his duty, in favor of doing other and contrary things which possess a greater emotional value to him. The religious man is religious in his actions, because his religious desires are stronger than his irreligious ones. He finds a greater satisfaction and content in religious actions than in the pursuits of the worldly-minded.*

"*The moral man is moral because his moral desires are stronger than his immoral ones. He obtains a greater degree of emotional satisfaction and contentment in being moral than in being immoral. Everything we do is prompted by DESIRE in some shape or form, high or low. Man cannot be without desire and still act one way or another; or in any way whatsoever. DESIRE is the motive factor behind all thoughts and action—it is a natural law of life.*"

From the above passage you can see how *desire precedes thoughts and ACTION*. You always do what you want, imagine, or try to do. Now these statements may seem at first to be overly simplistic; but I mention them to emphasize that—in both our subjective and subconscious minds—we often fail to act along certain lines because (1) the <u>desire</u> is simply not there; or (2) the <u>desire</u> is purposely stifled or rejected by our <u>thoughts.</u>

Then we often re-gender questionable thoughts, push back scarred and fanciful desires into the closets of our mind, and ponder why we fail to reach our objectives or to "find ourselves" in real life. How, then, can you work to build correct and sustainable desire? This is largely accomplished by concentrating on *visualizing* your legitimate goals and allowing your subconscious mind to take over in the living room of your senses.

Reason all you want with your subconscious mind, and you'll find yourself still motivated by your emotions. <u>Two of the seven positive emotions are *desire* and *sex*</u>—neither to be culturally comingled with the satanic term, *lust*. The desire for sex is subsequently a rightful God-given *thought* process registering almost consistently in the minds of the most of us—advancing youth, middle agers, and elders alike. Positive thinking seniors—many no longer with a mate—must deal with imagined sexual thoughts that threaten their spiritual beliefs and social contentment. Unrestrained sexual language and unbridled intimate relationships can lead to a loss of friends and create enemies for seniors, threatening their reputation and their position in society. Despite the positive nature of these emotions, outward expressions of thought and actions regarding *desire* and *sex* are best kept within degrees of privacy and are not advised, particularly for seniors. Your negative emotions should be pushed to the cellars of both your subjective and subconscious minds.

If, during high school and college, you wanted to be an opera singer, and your father argued convincingly that you would make a better lawyer, you may have been convinced against your will; but the desire would linger still. The reason you did not act upon that desire was due to *fear* and *disbelief*. If you were still trying to find your chief aim in life, you would first have to begin building desire. This determined action requires, first, elimination of the seven basic fears (Death, Old Age, Ill Health, Pain, Lost Love, Poverty, and Criticism) and any subsidiary fears that may be holding you back; secondly, you would have to build *belief* as the mainstay of your desire. As with desire, belief is built largely through visualization or *autosuggestion*, wherein you influence the subconscious through the steps mentioned earlier.

You may *desire* a pretty maiden of a friend; but *disbelief, moral thoughts*, or *physical reality,* can discourage further action. Decide upon the belief you want (the maiden) and set the objective firmly in your subconscious mind. In the vestibule of religion and reality, your subconscious will likely choose intellect over moral defect, and the thought will become weeds to cut in your subjective mind.

In short, begin to see, hear, smell, touch, live, your goals and chief objectives in life. Believe that you will receive rewards and accomplishments; then shut the door on every suggestion of fear, worry, or failure. Unrealistic fanciful thoughts and fears are the bastion of limitation. Worried about age? A Stanford psychologist said that *"The sweet spot for happiness arrives in the late 60s to early 70s."* See the rightful things you want as already yours. Believe it. Dream it. Go out and accomplish it, by following the prescribed procedure below for influencing the subconscious mind. Don't worry about things that have happened to you in the past. Perhaps you've failed before, and you fear criticism or poverty. Misfortune must always stay in your past and never be allowed to hinder the future.

Remember that those who like to criticize others are likely to be failures themselves; and failures, like other forms of misery, love company. Instead of bemoaning your past, *visualize* yourself as on the next rung of the ladder, and the next step above that one, and upward toward the rewards and goals you have set firmly in your mind.

Older people are often stereotyped as "stodgy" characters burdened down with chronic illness and disabilities when, in fact—and contrary to popular myth—you can climb the ladder of success at whatever rung you are on in life, relative to your age. The process for all ages usually requires an initial period of putting all of your eggs in one basket at an optimal point in time so that your energies are not dissipated by sidelines. Here's what Andrew Carnegie had to say about the concentration of your efforts toward a *specific aim* in life: "Place your eggs in one basket and see that no one kicks it over."

Obviously Mr. Carnegie made this remark *with tongue in cheek*, since having a fall-back career field can be a wise decision; but you cannot spend time worrying that others might kick over your only basket; nor can you be plagued by mental conflicts, fears, and tensions brought about by suspicions, or by any of the negative emotions. When you finally understand that the aim of life is not the accumulation of material rewards, but to live life to its fullest, your mind will then cease to concern itself excessively with the external world. And from the time you plant a *definite chief aim* in your mind, your mind begins, both consciously and unconsciously, to accumulate and store away the material that you need to reach your principal goals in life. Never forget this cardinal rule of success:

You may have anything you want, or be anything you want, providing you know exactly what you want, want it hard enough, confidently expect to attain it, persistently determine to attain it, and are willing to pay the price for its attainment..

Everything in this world that *man* has produced began as a thought. Sometimes we act quickly on the thought; other times we have to wait for favorable conditions. There is no such thing as "luck." *Everything* is the *result* of some cause.

The source of all power on all planes—physical, mental, emotional—is God, or the Universal Mind. Your *Subjective Mind* link can bring you ANYTHING which is not prohibited by time and space.

STATEMENT OF PHYSICAL GOALS
(Sample)

(It is wise to begin with just a few main goals and aim for the sun.)

- **On or before (*month/day/year*) I will have (*amount*)** in the bank which I will earn in varying amounts and deposit accordingly.
- By (long-term date) I will have (*amount*) in the bank and will begin to invest half of it in (*form of investment*).
- My income in (*timeframe*) will be at least (*desired amount*).
- By (*date*) I will resign my job and go to work with (*name*), whose office is located at (*address*). By (*date*) I will have developed a promotional idea for the sale of (*product*) which will lead to a partnership or self-sufficiency.
- By (*date*) I will begin my retirement and be free from debts.

> On or before *(date)* I will have sold my house for a minimum of *(amount)* and moved to *(destination)*.

> By *(date)* I will have lost *(pounds)* and quit the habit of *(hang up or addiction)*.

> By *(date)* I will travel to *(destination)*.

> By *(date)* I will enroll in (name of *school or educational institute*).

> By *(date)* I will own a *(luxury item)*.

> By *(date)* I will hire a maid or house cleaner.

> By *(date)* I will begin lessons in (*activity, skill,* or *self-improvement*).

Now that you have written down your *physical goals*, it should be evident to you that you must render something in return for their fulfillment. You have asked for substantial rewards. What are you prepared to promise and deliver in return for the achievement of these goals?

All of us have certain unused latent talents, skills, and capabilities which, in effect, amount to untapped energies. Think for a moment of your own hidden energy sources. Take inventory in your mind. This act—*taking mental stock of yourself*—is the first of three steps you must take to apply the power of *suggestion*. Your second step is to deliver this inventory to your subconscious mind through the *written and spoken word*. Write down your talents, skills, and capabilities, and orally promise to deliver them in return for the fulfillment of your goals. Your <u>third step</u> in utilizing the power of *suggestion* is to take *action*.

Your body can be likened to a river—sometimes placid, then flowing swiftly into rapids, and finally plunging into a deep gorge, where the swirling water is tamed and released for its peaceful journey to the great ocean. Think of all the wasted energy if the river is not used to power generators, which, in turn, supply you with an even greater source of energy—electricity. I make this comparison to emphasize the importance of *action* in the achievement of your goals. It will not be enough to write down your goals and repeat them to yourself if you are not prepared to follow through. *The power of suggestion will not take hold of your life until you commit yourself to ACTION.*

Take time to deliberate; but when the time for action arrives, stop thinking and go to war; and your problems and troubles begin to disappear. All great men are men of quick decision which flows from their intuitions, their accumulated knowledge, and previous experience. And the woman who is resolved to be respected can make herself to be so, even amidst an army of soldiers. All of us can relate stories of men and women who have accomplished great things in their short lives. Upon close examination of these lives, we see that their great accomplishments were achieved with a concentration of effort, that—to idle spectators whose goals were ill-defined—looked like they were almost impossible to actualize.

Those who have accomplished great things in life have understood and applied the power of *suggestion*. And since *suggestion* is the handmaiden to *enthusiasm*—a vital component in the science of influencing yourself and others—you can understand how rich and powerful personalities have achieved their substantial goals. A word diagram follows which summarizes at a glance the process required to implement your goal plan:

> **Thoughts / Words / Action** = Suggestion > Enthusiasm = **Influence Over Others**

Once the above correlation is understood, you can then draft a statement similar to the one below, wherein you promise services in exchange for the fulfillment of your physical goals. Unbelief, rejection, or denial of these statements can result in inaction and failure. Faith must come from the soul. **The *Statement of Exchange* can be brief and should be written out and read aloud immediately after repeating your *Statement of Physical Goals*.** It is a truism that what we wish for hard enough, we soon believe we will achieve. And when you've learned to draw on your subconscious powers, there's really no limit to what you can accomplish. Emerson said, **"All I have seen teaches me to trust the Creator for all I have not seen."**

STATEMENT OF EXCHANGE
(See Rule #4)

In exchange for these rewards, I will perform to the best, highest, and fullest of my ability for the benefit of those receiving my services as (whatever your calling, position, or status in life). I believe that I will achieve these goals. Their accomplishment will come to me in proportion to my efforts expended to achieve these goals. I will recognize these opportunities when they are presented to me. And I will act on them when they are achieved. I accept the loan of thankfulness and all benefits given to me; and I will repay that loan by bringing happiness and humble service to others less fortunate than myself.

Now that you have written down both statements, keep them handy at all times until you have committed them to memory. Revise and upgrade the statements when new goals are needed, when old ones are accomplished, and when the nature of your services changes in any way. Refer to these statements at least twice a day, preferably before you go to sleep at night, and again in the morning. Remember, this must be done orally. These statements should be your constant companions; treat them as you would new born children—give them the attention they need, and the absolute care, handling, and effort they demand.

MONEY LESSON LEARNED: Money and time are the heaviest burdens in life, and the unhappiest of mortals are those who have more of either than they know how to use.

Chapter 16
SCRIPT and FLA(M)E RULE #14
Go the Extra MILE

One of the most common causes of failure is the habit of quitting when one is overtaken by temporary defeat. James J. Corbett, the famous boxer and former heavyweight champ, once made these remarks about the value of *going the extra mile* when your mind and body tell you it's time to quit: "Fight one more round. When your feet are so tired that you have to shuffle back to the center of the ring, fight one more round. When your arms are so tired you can hardly lift your hands to come out on guard, fight one more round. When your nose is bleeding and your eyes are black and you are so tired that you wish your opponent would crack you one more time on the jaw and put you to sleep, fight one more round—remembering that the man who always fights one more round is never whipped." Remember your phone call that was never returned? Try again. Perseverance and audacity generally win.

There are many sound reasons for turning in a performance that is not required and which may not return to you an immediate reward. But perhaps the most persuasive reason for *going the extra mile* is that, on balance, once you have acquired the habit you will outdistance the rest of the pack and claim a greater success. Your reward could come in the form of material gain and/or public acclaim, along with the personal satisfaction you receive from knowing you've done your best. People admire those with a smack of age who relish the saltiness of time. If you are now retired from your job or profession, you can even *go the extra mile* by turning the twilight of a retirement scenario into a re-adjustment toward daylight in your life.

You are familiar with the worker—let's say a male—who performs only as much as he is paid for; no more; sometimes less. Since there is nothing outstanding in his performance, there is nothing about him that will attract favorable comment. Whatever rewards he receives are based, not on merit, but solely on seniority. He gains only by default. And surely no one will recognize him as a winner in life. Consider, then, the worker who goes *the extra mile*. He stands out from those around him, and he is much in demand. Everyone seeks out his services because they realize he will yield to them a bonus in terms of his work performance. If you are in business for yourself, and you've acquired the habit **of *going the extra mile***, you will end up paying the bonus to yourself, and this can be reflected in greater success and monetary reward for you. The person who has adopted the habit **of *going the extra mile*** also finds that he or she is immune to failure, because they have chosen a better position, where the sun is behind their back. When others have given up and fallen by the wayside, the undefeated person continues the extra mile toward their goal. There is an unexplained law in nature that appears to yield benefits in greater measure than the effort put forth. If you try to get something for nothing, you will end up less than even—you will eventually lose out. Employers who abuse or violate this law are penalized by the loss of valuable employees. And the self-employed are chastened for channeling rewards from their extra efforts into selfish and illegitimate pursuits—this through life reversals such as criminal activity, ill health, disharmony at home, loss of friends, lack of spirituality, or eventual self-destruction.

To test this law for yourself, you need only devote a half hour or an hour of your time each day to the performance of duties or services for which you cannot see reward. This action could involve activities in your family, at work, or services within the outreach of your church. The very fact that you are conscious of this principle will help it to become a habit in your life. You will be ultimately compensated. You need not be burdened with worry that your efforts will not in some way be given the recognition they deserve, plus a bonus. For a thorough understanding of this principle, I refer you to Emerson's *Essay on Compensation*, which explains duality in every act in nature:

POOR WORK = POOR PAY

EQUAL WORK = EQUAL PAY

EXTRA WORK = EXTRA PAY

Now you can point to the unemployment compensation laws, slave labor, and to the welfare laws, and claim that Emerson's "Law" is not valid. However, this is not the case, since every act is not always ***immediately*** rewarded or penalized. On balance, those who irrationally seek or receive something for nothing are the big losers in life, since they are continually in debt to the unseen world of nature through its "law" of compensation.

Going the extra mile, too, means helping others to get ahead, since it is not possible for you to become a happy and truly successful person without extending a helping hand to others. This is a difficult principle for some achievers to understand, because advice is often promulgated that you should look out for yourself first, so as not to be put down or put upon by others. The confusion here lies between foolishness and wisdom. Once you understand the definition of a fool, you have no need for the *"look out for yourself" philosophy."*

A fool may be known by six things: anger, without cause; speech, without profit; change, without progress; inquiry without object; putting trust in a stranger, and; mistaking foes for friends. -- Arab proverb

It is not foolish to put yourself ahead in the world by first helping others to get ahead. It is, however, foolish to allow yourself to be continually stepped on. Foolish acts are penalized, never rewarded. Forgiveness, sympathy, and love are the emotions of a wise person; whereas selfishness, suspicion, and avarice are the coveted emotions of fools. Take time, then, from your aspirations for a successful life to *go the extra mile* by helping others as you would expect the same from the best of them. You will be the ultimate beneficiary of your kind and charitable works.

MONEY LESSON LEARNED: The love of money is the root of all evil; which while some coveted after they have erred from the faith, and pierced themselves through with many sorrows. *–1 Timothy 6:10*

B.K. HAYNES

HOW THINK YE?

Then came Peter to Jesus and said, Lord how oft shall my brother sin against me, and I forgive him? till seven times?

Jesus saith unto him, I say not unto thee, Until seven times: but, Until seventy times seven.

Therefore, is the kingdom of heaven likened unto a certain king, which would take account of his servants.

And when he had begun to reckon, one was brought unto him, which owed him ten thousand talents.

But forasmuch as he had not to pay, his lord commanded him to be sold, and his wife, and children, and all that he had, and payment to be made.

The servant therefore fell down, and worshipped him, saying, Lord, have patience with me, and I will pay thee all.

Then the lord of that servant was moved with compassion, and loosed him, and forgave him the debt.

But the same servant went out, and found one of his fellowservants, which owed him an hundred pence: and he laid hands on him, and took him by the throat, saying, Pay me that thou owest.

And his fellow servant fell down at his feet, and besought him, saying, Have patience with me, and I will pay thee all.

And he would not: but went and cast him into prison, till he should pay the debt.

So when his fellow servants saw what was done, they were very sorry, and came and told unto their lord all that was done.

Then his lord, after that he had called him, said unto him, O thou wicked servant, I forgave thee all that debt, because thou desiredst me:

Shouldest not thou also have had compassion on thy fellow servant, even as I had pity on thee?

And his lord was wroth, and delivered him to the tormentors, till he should pay all that was due unto him.

So likewise shall my heavenly Father do also unto you, if ye from your hearts forgive not every one his brother their trespasses.

Matthew 18: 21-35

Chapter 17
SCRIPT and FLAM(E) RULE #15
Act with ENTHUSIASM

Enthusiasm is the key to action. Every man, woman, and child on earth has *enthusiasm* at times; and when that spirit takes hold, the task is done, the point is made, and that person's influence over others is measured with greater weight. An effective sales presentation requires enthusiasm, and you'll observe this fact whether you are buying a new car or hearing a sermon.

Let's consider these two concerns in your life—one involves the physical and material position; the other deals with your spiritual requirements. You are more apt to respond favorably to either pitch if it is made with enthusiasm, because, at that moment, you are filled with belief, the mainstay of desire. So many times, however, our desire wanes when *enthusiasm* is down. It should be obvious that if you could be *enthusiastic* all your life, you could certainly influence a lot more people than you could now. But more importantly, since belief springs from *enthusiasm*, you will find yourself believing that you can and will accomplish all the things you set out to do.

Benjamin Franklin tracked his *enthusiasm* daily by recording in a notebook his progress toward mastering the virtues. Frank Bettger (*How I raised Myself From Failure to Success in Selling*) followed Franklin's practice by recording on note cards his daily level of *enthusiasm*. Human resources and spiritual powers, it seems, are given to those who use what resources and powers they have. Self-discipline and faith (belief in the Creator or in a spiritual power higher than yourself) are available to everyone. Use these resources and powers to become more *enthusiastic* in your own life. The penalty for *not* using them is apathy, inaction, and prolonged failure.

In his book, *The Secrets of Mind Power*, Harry Lorayne, the hypnotist, suggests how to make yourself more *enthusiastic* through self-hypnosis or *autosuggestion*: "Hypnotic suggestion is merely making the subject believe implicitly that he or she is something he isn't (more *enthusiastic*) or that the person can do something of which they ordinarily would not be capable (earning a million)."

The process of *autosuggestion* has already been explained to you. You need only to add to your daily statement your intent to show more *enthusiasm*. Since nothing great is ever achieved without *enthusiasm*, including winning the grand prize lottery, it is not likely that you will reach your goals or realize your chief aim in life without concentrated effort to master the success principle of acting *enthusiastically*. However, be aware of the fact that you are only human and that humans are not respected if they say one thing and do another; or if they abruptly change their demeanor from being a wall flower to suddenly parading around like an elephant in the room.

A springboard to mastering *enthusiasm* is through keeping in your mind a daily record of your *enthusiasm* level. If you find it low, then concentrate on raising the bar. Of course, if you're in sales, the ministry, politics, or the performing arts, you may not need this daily reminder to act *enthusiastically*. *Enthusiasm*, so to speak, comes with the territory. And since every act carries with it a commensurate penalty or reward, a lack of enthusiasm in these fields would immediately be penalized by inattention, disinterest, loss of faith, forfeiture of sales and votes, empty seats, and reduced income.

The difficulty most people have with building enthusiasm is in generating the necessary "belief" power to make it work. If you find yourself in a field of work for which you are ill suited, and you try to be enthusiastic about your job, you would doubtlessly make some progress. But you would stall out and have to crank yourself up again and again. This is true because you would not have persuaded yourself—and subsequently your subconscious mind—that your *enthusiasm* is genuine.

Remember Napoleon Hill's axiomatic statement:

<u>Whatever the human mind can conceive,</u>
<u>the human mind can achieve.</u>

If in your mind you cannot legitimately conceive of yourself as being *enthusiastic* about something, you will not believe it; nor, subsequently can you achieve it. *Conviction, faith, and belief, are all required for sustained enthusiasm.* Successful agers add these plus factors to their lives because they know that their good job, career, or situation may not be there tomorrow.

Many years ago I worked in the advertising department of a world-famous corporation. I had never wanted to work for big business; but nevertheless I was still floundering around searching for my life's career, and I called my judgment into question. After quitting my job, I purchased a few vending machines in expectation that they would afford me a small income and a measure of independence. I soon learned that the machines were situated in the worst possible locations for generating income. Despite this disappointment, my *enthusiasm* remained high because the machines represented a chance to become independent—a primary and totally believable goal. In consequence of this outlook, I proceeded to move the machines to more desirable and lucrative locations. I remember well how I accomplished this task and how I built up a very profitable small business from which I entered the limitless opportunity of real estate development.

When approaching the owners of various business establishments, I did not walk in and "beg" them for a location. My approach was always that I had the most "fantastic" money-making machine they had ever seen. My machine would pay them a higher rate of commission than those currently on their location; the machine did not threaten cash returns from the existing machines on site, because the commodity dispensed was not available to the customers of that establishment. My level of enthusiasm was so high that I often did not have to document consumer demand for the products. After a few minutes of persuasive discussion, the owner would say, "Well, if the machine is as good as you say, bring one around and we'll try it out." Once on location, I was usually there to stay.

Enthusiasm → Belief → Desire → Accomplishment

The aforementioned formula is a simplified version of how my goals were achieved. I became enthusiastic about something; I believed in it and caused others to share that belief; desire was created; I subsequently accomplished the task at hand. An enterprising individual knows, consciously or unconsciously, that he or she must be audacious and vigorous in his pursuit of goals. In essence, he or she begins with mere possibilities and converts them into probabilities. The heart of enterprise, then, is *enthusiasm*.

The most *enthusiastic* person who ever lived was Jesus Christ. We know this to be true because his influence has spread over more people throughout history than that of any person who ever lived. The very word, *enthusiasm* is derived from the Greek term signifying "God in us." Christians are taught to love God and to aspire to be like him through the spiritual process of being "born again."

The *Bible* says—if you—like Jesus—had God within you; and if you believed this dictum with utmost conviction and faith; and if you went about your effort to follow His will with the highest level of inspiration, zeal, dedication, and determination in repentance for your sins, you could change or reinforce your lifestyle for the greater good and achieve miracles. Spiritual *belief* arises from *enthusiasm*, as evangelists and preachers will attest. The *desire* to be "*saved*" and returned to Heaven as a child of God is an outgrowth of this Christian *belief*. For unhappy disbelievers, agnostics, atheists, and other religious skeptics, conversion to fundamental Christianity and the *enthusiastic* pursuit of its righteous *Biblical* liturgy could count in Heaven as the ultimate accomplishment in your search for spiritual balance and harmony during your remaining years on earth.

If you're not blessed with natural enthusiasm, how, then, can you acquire it? This question can be answered by asking yourself either or both of the following questions:

1. **Are you doing the work or rendering the service that you like best?**

2. **If not, do you have a definite chief aim in life toward which you are striving, and which will lead you to the work or situation of your choice?**

SCRIPT AND FLAME

If the answer to both questions is "no" you will have to develop a new career goal or a *definite chief aim* in life. In no other way can you begin to build enthusiasm and achieve happiness. Happiness, of course, is a state of mind; and no man is happy if he does not think himself so. However, if happiness to you means things like the home of your choice, money in the bank, vacations when you want to take them, prestige in your career field, and so on, then these things are vital ingredients of your *definite chief aim* in life. You can be become *enthusiastic* about these pleasures, even after your sixtieth year. An excerpt from Napoleon Hill's landmark work, *The Laws of Success*, follows:

"You may develop enthusiasm over your definite chief aim in life, whether or not you are in a position to achieve that purpose at the current time. You may be a long way from realization of your definite chief aim; but if you will kindle the fire of enthusiasm in your heart, and keep it burning, before long the obstacles that now stand in your way of your attainment of that purpose will melt away; and you will find yourself in the possession of power that you did not know you had."

I'll point out that *happiness* also lies in the future, not just in the past. You build enthusiasm by setting firm goals of achievement for yourself and working to see them fulfilled. But remember this adage for beginners: *Those who are enthusiastic to those who are not, are often something of a trial.*

A wise philosopher once said, *"Life is the only real counselor; wisdom unfiltered through your personal experience does not become a part of the moral tissue. And life will give you what you ask from her, only if you ask long enough and plainly enough."*

Another philosopher reserved these words of temperance for those faces flushed with youth, and for the grained faces of those who are *Heaven* bound:

"Age is opportunity no less than youth itself, though in another dress, and as the evening twilight fades away the sky is filled with stars, invisible by day." — Longfellow

How small a portion of our lives are the times that we really enjoy. In youth we are looking forward to things that are to come; in old age we are looking backward to things that are long gone; in manhood, though we appear indeed to be occupied in things that are present, we even then seem too often absorbed in vague determination to be vastly happy on some future date, *when we have time*. If you love life, you would be wise to follow Benjamin Franklin's example and not squander time, for that is the stuff of which life is made. Those who consistently achieve their goals in life understand too quickly that life is but an eternal day at most; while those who constantly fail, understand too late how long is our march to the grave.

MONEY LESSON LEARNED: There has never existed a money-laden and civilized society in which one portion did not live on the labor of the other.

Chapter 18
S(C)RIPT and FLAME RULE #16
Adopt the Spirit of <u>COURAGE</u>
as you Age

"Being over 70 is like being engaged in a war. All our friends are going or gone, and we survive amongst the dead and the dying as on a battlefield." – Murial Spark

Because the element of *Courage* is also used to describe and reference acts of bravery, we must first understand the difference between the two words. Without *Courage*—kindness and compassion are the tools of fools. *Courage*, along with self-sacrifice, discipline, and intelligence, are children of faith and vision.

Courage is the ability to undertake an overwhelming difficulty or severe sense of pain, despite the eminent and unavoidable presence of fear. We have discussed the necessity for overcoming this fear if we are to be successful in aging and other situations of struggle in life. Courage is a state of mind driven by a cause that makes any struggle worthwhile.

Bravery is the fuel of *courage* used to confront pain, danger, or attempts of intimidation without the victim feeling a sense of fear. It is strength in character that allows a person to always appear larger than the crisis, whether he or she is more powerful—with or without weapons or perceived physical ability—to tackle the struggle, regardless of the consequences. It is said that one man must always be willing to take upon himself the onus of evil, that other men may be spared greater evil. Moses died leaving to others the fruits of his mission in life. Think of such courage on earth before you are dead and gone.

The best hearts are ever bravest and the ones who dare to do more. Remember with great reverence, John Glenn – a U.S. Marine fighter pilot in World War II and in Korea; propelled to the hazardous role of test pilot in the 60's and then assigned to mount the perch of a life-threatening rocket as the first American astronaut to orbit the Earth; and thereafter appareled with grace in the pages of history as a 24-year member of Congress and later, at the age of 77, the oldest human to enter outer space, dead at 95 in 2016.

SCRIPT AND FLAME

The emphasis in this chapter is to *courageously* tackle the struggle of Good Old Age, while recognizing that our fears must also be overcome as we cultivate the habit of courage as we travel through life.

Bette Davis, the movie actress of yesteryear, is a perfect example of bravery fueling one woman's *courageous* and seemingly endless struggle against pain. In 1983, Ms. Davis underwent a double mastectomy for breast cancer; and two weeks later she suffered four strokes, followed soon thereafter by a broken hip. This relentless attack of pain shattered her body, mind, and soul within a single year. The courageous actress had this to say during her long period of recovery: "Old age ain't no place for sissies." She then left her sick bed to make several films, finally passing in 1989 at age 81.

As we age, we could find ourselves far from the maddening crowd and haunted by the deadly feel of loneliness. Successful aging means that we must press on in our physical lives and in our thoughts, believing that a better fate awaits us, despite our loss of strength and energy. If we can walk, then walk; if we can run, then run. Whatever your age, keep moving; and show care in your eyes, even from your wheelchair. Remember that one third of people 65 and over face falls in their lives and that 20 percent of elders with hip fractures die within a year; so keep up your courage and watch your step and attitude.

Remember that another dangerous weakness of elders who have become cheerful is to forget that they are no longer in good spirits, especially when taking a fall.

We are all aware of the courageous heroes of the world in peace and war. The media, movies, and books tell us so. And the best hearts are ever the bravest, whether rich or poor, young or old, gifted in the creative arts, or in all forms of human endeavor.

> Give me a young man in whom there is something of the old, and an old man in whom there is something of the young. Guided so, a man may grow old in body but never in mind. - Marcus Tullius Cicero (106-43 BC)

Following are revealing internet postings about courage from The *Courage* and Bravery of Elders – TIME GOES BY:

Posting 1

"Hey, if you all are gonna die someday, I want to die, too. I do NOT want to be the only human who never dies. Today is all any of us have. This is the day. . . enjoy and be glad in it. Even though our lifestyle is not as glorious as it was, life itself is still glorious and mysterious.

"I do not suffer now and worry about how much suffering lies ahead of me, but as a career nurse, I have seen so many little kids suffer far more at a young age than I do. . . so I do not whine, nor can I conclude that a life of suffering is a worthless life, or that suffering has no purpose. I know better than that. I'm grateful for every suffering human who has crossed my path or walked beside me, for they have given me courage for my own life.

"It is hard to see some of my friends die, but I go on making friends, and . . . some of them are through social media, yea, even blogging! I know none of us wants to become dependent, but as a nurse who has worked with the aged, I can tell you that, while it is true some caregivers really do mistreat old people, MOST do NOT mistreat old people. In fact, I think people are unusually kind to us as a rule. If ever I lay dependent in bed, peeing my undies, I hope I can remember the children who never could acquire bladder control and who never could stand before a crowd and speak. I hope I never take my suffering as a "personal insult" from the universe. I love life. O, ok, I'll admit it: I whine sometimes, but I'm not serious in my whining."

Posting 2

" I am not brave nor am I *courageous*. If my husband were to die I might just do away with myself the next day. On the other hand, I might find the strength to continue on. But I would be very afraid. I would not wish to impinge on my children's freedom or to drain their finances."

Posting 3

". . .Thank you Ronnie and readers for putting into words many things I only think to myself. I have been working on living in the moment. Very hard to do, but living in the past causes stress and in the future causes stress. So I pull myself back into the moment whenever I can. Also helping others is great to give a sense of usefulness to me. I try to find things to do as an act of kindness whenever I can. It is more of a challenge sometimes now that I need help of my own, but by no means impossible."

Posting 4

"I've never stopped to think in terms of bravery or *courage* where aging is concerned. I kind of mentally rehearse what I'd do if I were alone and dependent on others. As it is legally binding on families in Spain to care for their elders, there are few resources for those on their own. "For the first time ever, my partner indicated that whichever one of us survives the other, she should return to the UK and live our days out of our own language. Easy to say, difficult to accomplish if health is failing."

Posting 5

" My paternal grandmother lived to be 92; she suffered from crippling arthritis. . . yet kept going, even having a veggie garden up into her 70s."

Posting 6

"Since my mother lived to be 94 and my MIL is now 96, I have seen how age debilitates. And it's obvious that my MIL is "ready to go" as she herself says. But the fear that creeps up occasionally when thinking about old age needs to be replaced with the love that still exists and remains in our hearts. I really enjoyed your distinctions between bravery and courage."

Posting 7

The Scholar and the Saint: Two valiant men

"I am thinking today of two valiant old men, one a scholar, the other a saint, and what they teach us about how to live and die. They lived far apart in place and time; but they were united in their courage and in their sense of something greater than themselves for which they gave their lives.

"Today is the feast day of St. John Kemble, a Hereford man who became a priest and worked quietly among English and Welsh Catholics for fifty-four years until, in 1678, he was accused of being party to Titus Oates' so-called Popish Plot. He was tried and acquitted of involvement but subsequently condemned as a 'seminary priest'. "He was hanged, drawn and quartered on Widemarsh Common on 22 August 1679. Before he was executed, he said, 'I die only for professing the old Catholic religion, which was the religion that first made this kingdom Christian.' He was eighty 'tears' old.

"Every time I walk down Widemarsh Street or drive across the common, I remember St. John. I think of the barbarity of being hanged, drawn and quartered and being subjected to similar treatment by ISIS today. He and Khaled al-Assad, the Syrian archeologist murdered two days ago for refusing to reveal where some of Palmyra's treasures were hidden, were just a few months apart in age. Both were men of integrity and valour. Both were men with a clear sense of purpose; St. John saw his duty in upholding the faith of his fathers, Dr. al-Asaad in preserving the treasures of antiquity —and both paid the price of their convictions.

"We tend to consider old age as a kind of weakness. As our bodies begin to crumble and sometimes our minds too, we think uneasily of Shakespeare's sixth and seventh ages. Our life's work is done; it is time to accept the inevitable. Death is, of course, inevitable for all of us; but how we meet it, what we make of it, and what others draw from it, is not so predictable. St. John Kemble and Dr. Khaled al-Assad could both look back on lifetimes of achievement. Many of the missions St. John established lasted until the nineteenth century.

"Dr. al-Assad was 'Mr. Palmyra', the man who knew more about that important ancient city than any other. Yet it is arguable that their death, and the way in which they met it, was their finest hour, the crowning achievement of their lives. St. John refused to give up his religious faith and conform to the Church of England. Dr. al-Assad refused to break faith with his stewardship of historical artifacts and the duty of scholarship. They did not plead old age as an excuse, but met death clear-eyed and bravely. We may lack the courage of either; but we can surely be grateful for the example they gave to us."

A WORN PATH

Eudora Welty, the revered short story writer, lived for 92 years. Here is an abridged summary of her tale about the incredible of courage and bravery of a century-old

black woman, small and frail, and the travails of her long walk to a southern town in days gone by. Her name was Phoenix Jackson.

She carried a thin, small cane made from an umbrella as she followed a path through the pinewoods. Under her red rag dress, her hair came down in ringlets with an odor like copper. "Out of my way, all you foxes, owls, beetles, jack rabbits, coons," she hollered as she switched at the brush.

The path ran up a hill, "Seems like chains about my feet, time I get this far," she said. At the top of the hill she said, "Now down through the oaks," she said at length. At the bottom, a bush caught her dress. "Thorns, you just doin' your appointed work. Never want to let folks pass, no sir. Old eyes thought you was a pretty little green bush. Finally, trembling all over, she stood free, and after a moment dared to stoop for her cane. "Sun so high," she cried," thick tears over her eyes. "Time is gettin' all gone."

At the foot of the hill a log had been laid across the creek. Lifting her dress, and with her cane in front, she closed her eyes and tapped her way across the log; then, opening her eyes, she said, "I wasn't as old as I thought." She left the creek and had to creep and crawl under a barbed wire fence. She talked loudly to herself. "This late in the day I ain't gonna let my dress be torn or my leg be cut off if I be caught." Once through the fence, she came to a clearing where big dead trees, like black men, were standing in the withered cotton field. She saw a buzzard.

"Why you watchin' me?" she cried out. Then something tall, black, and skinny appeared before her, ragged and dancing in the field. "Ghost," she said, only to discover that it was a scarecrow.

She stumbled on through the whispering field, crossing a swamp where the moss hung as white as lace from every limb. "Sleep on, alligators, and blow your bubbles." Then the track went into the road. A black dog with a lolling tongue came out of the weeds by the ditch. She was meditating, and not ready, and when he came to her she only hit him a little with her cane. Over she went into the ditch. Down there, her senses drifted away. A dream visited her, "Old woman," she said to herself, "That black dog come up out of the weed to stall you off, and now he there sittin' on his fine tail, smilin' at you."

A white man finally came along and found her, a hunter, a young man with a dog on a chain. He lifted her up, gave her a swing in the air, and set her down. "Anything broken, Granny?" On your way home?"

"I bound to go my way mister. I thank you for your trouble." she said.

"How old are you, Granny?"

"There ain't no tellin', mister, No tellin'."

She walked on. In the paved town it was Christmas time. There were red and green electric lights crisscrossed everywhere. Moving slowly from side to side, she went into a big building and into a tower of steps to an office.

"Here I be," she said. There was a ceremonial stiffness over her body. "A charity case, I suppose," said an attendant who sat at the desk before her. "Speak up, Grandma," the woman said. Old Phoenix only gave a twitch to her face as if a fly were bothering her. "Are you deaf?" cried the attendant. But then the nurse came in. "Oh, that's old Aunt Phoenix," she said. "She doesn't come for herself—She has a little grandson. She makes these trips as regular as clockwork."

"Now how old is the boy?" asked the nurse. Old Phoenix did not speak. But she only waited and stared straight ahead. "You mustn't take up our time this way, Aunt Phoenix," the nurse said. "Tell us quickly about your grandson, and get it over. He isn't dead, is he?"

At last there came a flicker and a flame of comprehension across her face, and she spoke. "My grandson, it was my memory had left me. There I sat and forgot why I made my long trip."

"Forgot?" the nurse frowned. "After you came so far?"

Then Phoenix was like an old woman begging a dignified forgiveness for waking up frightened in the night. "I never did go to school, I was too old at the Surrender," she said in a soft voice. "I'm an old woman without an education. It was my memory fail me. My little grandson, he just the same age, and I forgot it in the coming."

Phoenix spoke unmasked now, "No, missy, he not dead. He sit there in the house all wrapped up, waitin' by himself. We the only two left in this world. He suffer and don't seem to put himself back at all. He got a sweet look. He gonna last. I remembers so plain now. I not gonna forget him again, no, the whole endurin' time. I can tell him from all the others in creation."

"All right." The nurse was trying to hush her now. She bought her a bottle of medicine. "Charity," she said, making a check mark in a book.

"I thank you," she said.

"It's Christmas time, Grandma," said the attendant. Could I give you a few pennies out of my purse?"

"Five pennies is a nickel," said Phoenix stiffly.

"Here's a nickel," said the attendant.

She stared at her palm closely, with her head on one side. Then she gave a tap with her cane on the floor. "This is what come to me to do," she said. "I goin' to the store and buy my child a little windmill they sells, made out of paper. He gonna find it hard to believe there such a thing in the world. I'll march myself back where he is waitin', holdin' it straight up in his hand."

She lifted her free hand, gave a little nod, turned around, and walked out of the doctor's office. Then her slow step began on the stairs, going down.

> The most sublime courage I have ever witnessed has been among that class too poor to know they possessed it, and too humble for the world to discover it." –H. W. Shaw

SCRIPT AND FLAME

CREATIVE COURAGE IN GOOD OLD AGE

They say that Good Old Age now begins at 60. So when does the sun rise again at retirement? Some futurists predict a spring forward for agers into their "80's" extended daylight years. Medical and technological advances now offer bonus years of living for those pushing their youth into the 60s, 70s and 80s. Some people refuse to sit and growl from some shady corner of retirement. Doris Day was still as perky at age 92, as when she sang on the big band stage and waltzed into the Hollywood spotlight. After the death of her third husband and deeply in debt, she continued on her "Sentimental Journey" with a cheerful and positive attitude, forming the Doris Day Animal Foundation. "I like to stay active," she said. "I like to walk with my doggies."

In his book, CREATORS, renowned author and historian, Paul Johnson explains the fact that all of us—no matter our age—can, and do, create something in one way or another. We are all made in God's image, so creativity is in our genes; and the only problem is bringing it out.

A man or woman, in the autumn or winter of their lives, can create a business or a range of productive gardens. Humans of any age can create humor and jokes to make others happy. Johnson writes of the chancellor of Oxford, on the verge of his eighties, penning large-scale biographies and best sellers of Gladstone and Churchill.

A Study by the Kauffman Foundation, that surveyed 652 U.S.-born CEOs and heads of product development, revealed that the number of businesses created by those over 50 years of age doubled the number of those start-up enterprises of those younger than 25. And it is known that people of all ages have elements of business and desire in their lives, such as it is, and that the master looks sharpest at his own business.

In fact, entrepreneurs seem to get better with age. Benjamin Franklin invented bifocals at age 76. Billionaire Carlos Slim (aged 73), perennially one of the richest people in the world, argues that workers in developed economies are in their prime during their 60's. The famous franchise of Kentucky Fried Chicken was started by Colonel Harlan Sanders at age 65. Jeanne Dowell spent over 40 years teaching yoga; then, in 2008—at 80 years young—she sought her pleasure by founding Green Buddha clothing.

Authors, like coins, grow dear as they grow old. Laura Ingalls Wilder, author of Little House on the Prairie, did not publish her first book, Big Woods, until she was well into her 60's. And there is no author so poor, and whose heart is ever more at our service, than Frank McCourt, the Irish-American teacher, who suffered the pangs of poverty and who did not achieve literary acclaim until he became—at 66—a best seller and winner of the Pulitzer Prize for his book, Angela's Ashes.

Creative courage can also force you to struggle when there is little or no hope; to live when life's salt is gone; to dwell in the shadow of a precious dream; to endure; and to still proceed with calmness. Aging can grow darker as we go on, until only one light is left shining on us; and that is faith, both in God and in life's mission.

Consider the lives of those renowned personalities of old who left astounding legacies only to be confronted with difficult times. Author Robert Louis Stevenson, weakened with unreliable lungs, pressed on with few days to live, limited working hours, and huge willpower, to write such master pieces as *Dr. Jekyll and Mr. Hyde*, *Kidnapped*, *Treasure Island*, and *The Master of Ballantrae*.

Richard Wagner, the famous composer, squandered his wealth and had to beg for cash. Beethoven struggled against deafness; and his letters reveal his profundity for cash donations. He finally escaped from the furnace on earth and reached out for the hand of God. Walt Disney is said to have needed to wash his hands, sometimes thirty times within the hour. And Charles Dickens, after writing *David Copperfield*, is said to have slipped into a frenzy that reduced him to reading his own works rather than creating new literary material. The absence of love in the lives of many distressed authors has been traced to loneliness. True wisdom, it appears, comes from the overcoming of suffering and sin.

The legacy of Sister Elizabeth Kenny, who revolutionized the treatment of polio through physical therapy, reveals that, in her later years, she was finally memorialized as the most admired woman in the world—her treatment method having successfully cured thousands of sufferers from the disease, including such movie stars as Alan Alda, Martin Sheen, and Dinah Shore. Another exemplary recount of courage is the legendary "Lady in Gray," Florence Nightingale, who, at the age of 82, became sick and forcefully exchanged her position in the bed with her nurse, then remarking at age 90, just before she died, "I am watching at the altar of murdered men, and I shall be fighting their cause."

Angela Lansbury, the ageless and brilliant screen star, summed up the issue of controlling your own destiny, with the remark that, ". . . when you've learned to draw on your subconscious powers, there's really no limit to what you can accomplish." Harriet Beecher Stowe, the acclaimed Black author of *Uncle Tom's Cabin*, said she wrote the story after seeing visions in her mind. To her dying day she insisted that the author was actually God. Little was known in the heat of the Civil War era about a subconscious mind.

Norman Vincent Peale, the renowned minister and author of *The Power of Positive Thinking*, had this to say about the rule of thoughts: "Change your thoughts and change the world." He left us with this insightful story about a man of 80-odd-years, who found great pleasure in the web of life, never thinking of age as a tyrant. When his brother died, he received a tin box filed with well-worn pages and a family *Bible*, learning that his birth date had actually granted him perhaps 13 more years—that the pleasurable brother still alive was actually 93 years of age. Staring at the date, he was shaken by the thought of growing old. He felt healthy and was the happiest creature living. Now he was suddenly 93 years old. He stopped working around the house. Neighbors brought him food. In six months he was dead.

Thoughts, as we know, are unconscious visions or words that can develop into reality. Vibrations in our mind of ugly aging, empathy, anger, or hatred often spill out and resonate into actions, some of which can hurt us. Your resolute will to control your own mind and destiny is a safety valve in your character. <u>You are responsible for your thoughts as well as your actions</u>. Consider this about the poverty of our minds: Some say that most people use only five percent of their mental potential; others claim that perhaps the right number is 20%, leaving an abundance of unused mind power, most of which can be developed into positive thoughts.

This book was written while recovering from a difficult surgery on a third joint implant; and the publication is perhaps—*in terms of the subject matter and the telepathic transplant of related positive thoughts for mankind from a higher power*—the equivalent benefit of this recent setback of pain in my life; and as Shakespeare would have it: "Let me not so much as to say, am I getting better of my pain? as am getting better for it?" . . .Yes I am.

Remember this remark from the *School of Love*: "It is not the abundance of knowledge that satisfies the soul, but to feel and relish things externally."

In trying to give my family what peace and security is left in the world, I have deeded my home and the remainder of my farm to my son and his family and am pursuing other interests at this time; and though the transfer of a home and acres can be bestowed, an inheritance of knowledge and wisdom cannot. The wealthy man can pay others for doing his work and carrying on his business; but it is physically impossible to transfer enlightenment or to purchase any kind of self-culture.

Thoughts are dreams until they can be turned into action; and, in essence, there is nothing good or bad in a world of random and uncontrolled thought; only thinking makes it so. So as I race past the 80's in my age I will continue to explore the power *of accurate thought* and the magic of the human mind.

"As for man, his days are grass; as a flower in the field, so he flourisheth. For the wind passeth over it, and it is gone; and the place thereof shall know it no more" – Psalm of David

In conclusion, I want to repeat three important observations about all colors of success made at the beginning of this discussion:

1. **An intangible impulse of thought can be transmuted into material rewards by the application of known principles.**

2. Knowledge is only potential power. It becomes power only when and if it is organized into definite plans of action and definite ends.

3. It is never too late to use these 16 RULES laid out in the chapters of this book to advance your life. You may not be proficient with all of them; and you will stumble over others. The losses in my career can be directly traced to those rules I neglected to follow.

And remember the good old days:

Can man be so age-stricken that no faintest sunshine of his youth may visit him once a year? It is impossible. The moss on our time-worn mansion brightens into beauty; the good old pastor, who once dwelt here, renewed his prime and regained his boyhood in the genial breeze of his ninetieth spring. Alas for the worn and heavy soul, if whether in youth or age. It has outlived its privilege of springtime sprightliness -- Hawthorne

MONEY LESSON LEARNED: Should we not be ashamed to heap up the greatest amount of money and care little about wisdom and truth and the greatest improvement of the soul?

A TREASURE SCROLL OF THE 16 SUCCESS RULES

1. Develop the <u>Savings</u> Habit
2. Learn the Art of <u>Accurate</u> Thinking
3. Have <u>Confidence</u> in Yourself
4. Master the Art of <u>Self Control</u>
5. Master the Power of <u>Concentration</u>
6. Act to <u>Cooperate</u> with Others
7. Practice the <u>Golden Rule</u>
8. Use your <u>Imagination</u>
9. Develop a Pleasant <u>Personality</u>
10. Practice <u>Tolerance</u> and Patience
11. Learn to Profit from <u>Failure</u>
12. Learn to <u>Lead</u> and Harmonize with Others
13. Have a Definite Chief <u>Aim</u> in Life
14. Go the Extra <u>Mile</u>
15. Act with <u>Enthusiasm</u>
16. Adopt the Spirit of <u>Courage</u>

Chapter 19
ACTION POINTS

1. To meet life's challenges, memorize the 16 SCRIPT and FLAME success rules and repeat them to yourself orally until they have been firmly imbedded in your mind. *Learn the riches of saving money*. (RULE #1)

2. Study the 13 listed *inaccurate thought* patterns; and destroy, in your mind, the build-up of these known enemies to *accurate thought*. (RULE #2)

3. To determine the accuracy of your thought patterns, review and answer the listed 50 questions. (RULE #2)

4. Memorize and commit to habit the SELF-CONFIDENCE formula contained in the word, **A-D-M-I-T**. (RULE #3)

5. Develop a thorough understanding of the SEVEN BASIC FEARS and learn to defeat them in your mind. (RULE #4)

6. Renew an awareness of the four essential components of your life and practice them daily to keep them in balance. (RULE #4)

7. Understand the 7 Positive Emotions, and eliminate the 7 Negative Emotions from your thought processes. (RULE #4)

8. Write out a STATEMENT OF YOUR GOALS and constantly repeat these objectives until they are realized or altered. (RULE #4)

9. On a daily basis, cultivate and apply the steps required to master the power of CONCENTRATION. (RULE #5)

10. Choose and get to know—in your present state of body and mind—the six indispensable and invisible guards who can advance your leadership role and help you build character in any "master-mind" alliance. You can use Wikipedia for information and photos of admirable figures and personalities, both present and past. (RULE #6)

11. Commit the 10 BASIC MOTIVES to memory and develop a thorough understanding of them. (RULE #7)

SCRIPT AND FLAME

12. A runaway imagination can be self-defeating; therefore, memorize and understand the thoughts about *DESIRE*. (RULES #8 and #13)

13. Memorize and commit to habit the 12 steps for developing a PLEASANT PERSONALITY. (RULE #9)

14. Reread the essay, *Father Forgets* until you can promptly call upon its wisdom when impatience strikes. (RULE #10)

15. Reread Ralph Waldo Emerson's *Essay on Compensation*, explaining the duality that underlies the nature and condition of man. (RULE #14)

16. Work to purge yourself of any of the *50 Basic Failure Habits*.(Rule #11)

17. To spur your own initiative, develop a habit of answering *yes* to the three basic questions on LEADERSHIP. (RULE #12)

18. Get to know and practice the accumulation of life's true rewards. (RULE #12)

19. Judge yourself as being *good, fair, or poor* in each of the effective leadership qualities. Ask someone to give you a rating. (RULE #12)

20. **Prepare a Statement of Physical goals** and your **Statement of Exchange** following the eight steps for influencing the subconscious mind. If you've left out any steps, now is the time for revisions. (RULE #13)

21. Begin devoting some time every day toward the performance of duties or services (no matter how small) for which you cannot see immediate reward. (RULE #14)

22. Memorize and understand the Arabian proverb about fools. (RULE #14)

23. Build into your daily Statement your vow to be more *enthusiastic*. If you have not done so, include in this vow your intent to practice each of the other success principles as well. (RULE #15)

24. Memorize and understand the ENTHUSIASM formula in RULE #15.

25. Reread posting #7—The Scholar and The Saint: to understand courage in Good Old Age (Rule #16)

26. Any of mankind who would pass the evening of life with honor and comfort should, when young, one day become old—and REMEMBER when they are old, that they once were young. – (RULE OF LIFE)

SCRIPT AND FLAME

SHARE THIS BOOK WITH FRIENDS AND FAMILY

(Cut and paste Memory Card)

S **C** **R** **I** **P** **T**
Save Cooperate Rule Imagine Personality Tolerance
  Confidence
  Control
  Concentration
  Courage

ADMIT = <u>A</u>utosuggestion - <u>D</u>efinite Chief Aim - <u>M</u>ind Power - <u>I</u> Can - <u>T</u>ruth and Justice

F **L** **A** **M** **E**
Failure Lead Aim Extra Mile Enthusiasm
    Accurate Thinking

S **C** **R** **I** **P** **T**
Save Cooperate Rule Imagine Personality Tolerance
  Confidence
  Control
  Concentration
  Courage

ADMIT = <u>A</u>utosuggestion - <u>D</u>efinite Chief Aim - <u>M</u>ind Power - <u>I</u> Can - <u>T</u>ruth and Justice

F **L** **A** **M** **E**
Failure Lead Aim Extra Mile Enthusiasm
    Accurate Thinking

S **C** **R** **I** **P** **T**
Save Cooperate Rule Imagine Personality Tolerance
  Confidence
  Control
  Concentration
  Courage

ADMIT = <u>A</u>utosuggestion - <u>D</u>efinite Chief Aim - <u>M</u>ind Power - <u>I</u> Can - <u>T</u>ruth and Justice

F **L** **A** **M** **E**
Failure Lead Aim Extra Mile Enthusiasm
    Accurate Thinking

Appendix 1
SUMMARY OF MONEY LESSONS

1. Save 10% of what you earn; but not at the cost of liberality. Have the soul of a king and the hand of a wise economist. Chapter 3

2. Accurately assess your expenditures. Don't let your desires eat up your savings. Chapter 4

3. Great fortunes are not built in a day, but come as dollars adding themselves to those saved. Chapter 5

4. Make your money multiply and work for you. Ready money is Aladdin's lamp. Chapter 6

5. Let wise men hold money in their heads for you. You keep money in your heart. Chapter 7

6. Cooperate with others to own your own home. Keep money lenders away from your door. Chapter 8

7. He that wants money, means, and content is without three good friends. – *Shakespeare* Chapter 9

8. Cultivate the talent, training, and assistance you need to increase your ability to earn. Be specific in your goals and aspirations. Chapter 10

9. Trust not your money with schemers and trickster personalities. Look for good character. Chapter 11

10. Money that comes quickly goes quickly away. Take care of your money as you would your time. Chapter 12

11. If you desire to help others with your money, make sure you will not bring unnecessary burdens on yourself. Chapter 13

12. Lead not yourself into the pit of hopeless debt where you may struggle vainly for years. Chapter 14

13. Money and time are the heaviest burdens in life, and the unhappiest of mortals are those who have more of either than they know how to use. Chapter 15

14. The love of money is the root of all evil; which while some coveted after they have erred from the faith, and pierced themselves through with many sorrows. – *Bible* Chapter 16

15. There has never existed a money-laden and civilized society in which one portion did not live on the labor of the other. Chapter 17

16. Should we not be ashamed to heap up the greatest amount of money and care little about wisdom and truth and the greatest improvement of the soul? Chapter 18

SCRIPT AND FLAME

Appendix 2

CASH FLOW SHEET

From the *FIVE LESSONS A MILLIONAIRE TAUGHT ME* – Richard Paul Evans

"Warren Buffet, the sagacious multibillionaire, learned the lesson of winning in the margins of early life. At the age of just fourteen, he bought forty acres of Nebraska farmland with money he made on his paper route and then rented the land. He also invested in soda pop and pinball machines and used his profits to make his first investment partnership. The rest, they say, is history." — Evans

"That man is the richest whose pleasures are the cheapest." — Thoreau

"Few men are both rich and generous; fewer are both rich and humble." — Manning

THE FIVE LESSONS

CASH FLOW SHEET
CASH FLOW FOR _____
DATE

INCOME	PLANNED	ACTUAL
Salary 1 (after taxes)	$	$
Salary 2 (after taxes)	$	$
Other Income	$	$
Other income	$	$
Other income	$	$
Total Income	$	$
EXPENDITURES		
Nest Egg (Min. 10% of total income)	$	$
Charitable Donations	$	$
Mortgage or Rent	$	$
Food	$	$
Utilities	$	$
Auto Payments	$	$
Misc. Auto Expense	$	$
Repair	$	$
Maintenance	$	$
Gas	$	$
Auto Insurance	$	$
Life Insurance	$	$
Home Owner's Insurance	$	$
Medical Insurance	$	$
Clothing	$	$
Debt Payments	$	$
Misc. Expenses	$	$
	$	$
Total Expenditures	$	$
Income Less Expenditures	$	$

The five lessons a Millionaire Taught Me About Life and Wealth

B.K. HAYNES

NET WORTH SHEET

From the *FIVE LESSONS A MILLIONAIRE TAUGHT ME* – Richard Paul Evans

"This, then is held to be the duty of the man of wealth: To set an example of modest, unostentatious living, shunning display or extravagance; to provide moderately for the legitimate wants of those dependent upon him; and, after doing so, to consider all surplus revenues which come to him simply as trust funds which he is called upon to administer." — Andrew Caregie

"I have never seen a Brinks truck following a hearse." — Ray Croc, McDonalds

"Use wealth wisely, so that even the undertaker mourns your passing." — Mark Twain

THE FIVE LESSONS

NET WORTH SHEET
AS OF _____
DATE

ASSETS Current Liquid Assets		Other Liabilities Current Liabilities	
Cash (on hand)	$_____	Charge Accounts	$_____
Checking Account	$_____	Credit Cards	$_____
Savings Account	$_____	Insurance Due	$_____
Certificates	$_____	Taxes Due	$_____
Money Owed you	$_____	Current Bills Due	$_____
Life Insurance	$_____	Line of Credit	
Stocks/Bond	$_____	Other_____	$_____
Mutual Fund Shares	$_____	Other_____	$_____
Precious Metals	$_____	Other_____	$_____
Other_____	$_____	Other_____	$_____
Other_____	$_____	Total Current Liabilities	
Total Current Assets	$_____		
FIXED ASSETS		**LONG TERM LIABILITIES**	
Home	$_____	Auto Loan #1	$_____
Automobiles	$_____	Auto Loan #2	$_____
Furniture	$_____	Installment Loan	$_____
Jewelry	$_____	Personal Loan	$_____
Personal Property	$_____	Mortgage Loan	$_____
Other_____	$_____	Other_____	$_____
Total Fixed Assets	$_____	Long Term Liabilities	
		Total Liabilities	$_____
DEFERED ASSETS			
Retirement Plan	$_____	Total Assets	$_____
I.R.A	$_____	Total Liabilities	$_____
Other_____		NET WORTH	$_____
Other_____	$_____		
Total Deferred Assets	$_____		
Total Assets	$_____		

Appendix 3
SUMMARY OF 16 RULES

Memorize the words, S-C-R-I-P-T and F-L-A-M-E. When faced with a problem or concern, "Google" your brain for the applicable rule. Review content for solutions.

a. THOUGHTFUL QUESTIONS OF ACCURATE THINKING

b. INACCURATE THOUGHT PATTERNS, WRONGFUL THOUGHTS AND LIFE'S TRUE REWARDS FOR SUCCESSFUL AGING

c. ESSENTIAL COMPONENTS OF LIFE — SEVEN POSITIVE AND NEGATIVE EMOTIONS

d. STATEMENT OF GOALS AND STATEMENT OF EXCHANGE

e. CONCENTRATION ESSENTIALS

f. MASTER-MIND ALLIANCE DESCRIPTION

g. SAMPLE "MASTER-MIND" ALLIANCE

h. KEY HUMAN MOTIVATIONAL POINTS

i. HABITS FOR CREATING BRAIN POWER

j. 50 MAJOR FAILURE HABITS

k. EFFECTIVE LEADERSHIP QUALITIES AND TEN BASIC MOTIVES

l. HOW TO INFLUENCE THE SUBCONSCIOUS MIND

APPENDIX 3a
THOUGHTFUL QUESTIONS
OF ACCURATE THINKING (Rule #2)

1. Do you too often erupt with unmerited anger at people, or in other ways lose unnecessary control of your emotions?

2. Do you *slander* and *condemn* people?

3. Do you seek *revenge* for any real or imagined injustices?

4. Do you often *lose your poise* under unfavorable circumstances?

5. Do you ever think that other people "owe" you a living, and that you "can't" accomplish what you want to do?

6. Do you find yourself constantly *bragging* and *boasting* to raise your self-esteem?

7. Do you often feel as if you *have* to do something immediately, without giving it sufficient thought?

8. Are you always *griping* and *complaining* about people and things?

9. Do you express *contempt* for new ideas, proposals, and changes prior to examination?

10. Do you often feel that your life is *hopelessly* in the hands of someone else?

11. Do you harbor and openly express any racial and non-violent religious *prejudices?*

12. Is your mind filled with *unjustified fear* about anything or anyone?

13. Do you think of yourself as an *expert on all subjects?*

14. Do you readily speak about the *faults* of others?

15. Are you *slow* to forgive, forget, and restore *positive* thoughts?

16. Are you always in a state of *tension, worry,* and *anxiety?*

17. Are you easily led by *ideologies* foreign to you and your country?

18. Are you constantly at *war* with your family and mankind?

19. Do you make *enemies* easily?

20. Do you *begrudge* having to share your blessings?

21. Do you *draw back* from expressing gratitude to God or man?

22. Do you express *opinions* without being in possession of the facts?

23. Do you allow *negative* thoughts to dominate your mind?

24. Do you allow your mind to drift, steering toward indefinite goals?

25. Are you unable to cope with *excess* in eating, drinking, and other unhealthy habits?

26. Do you *wink* at transactions which are profitable to you and harmful to someone else?

27. Do you *bemoan defeat* as anything but a temporary setback?

28. Do you often see other people as *uncooperative*?

29. Do you "*play dirty*" with adversaries?

30. Do you *doubt* the existence of a power greater than yourself—a power that is available to you if you seek it diligently?

31. Do you become *morbid* and *unglued* after disappointments?

32. Are you always *apologizing* for not doing your best?

33. Are you quick to *accuse* and *blame* others?

34. Do you keep the door to the *past* open in your mind?

35. Do you *discount* the existence of certain eternal truths about mankind in relationship to his environment?

36. Do you *rationalize* about getting into justified debt and take repayment lightly?

37. Do you make liabilities of adversities and defeats, rather than turning them into assets?

38. Are you unduly *disturbed* by panics and depression in the economy?

39. Do you often *wish* you were someone else?

40. Do you sense that certain classes of people *dislike* you?

41. Do you ever find yourself trying to live *someone else's life* for them?

42. Do you allow your mind to *run away* with thoughts of wealth?

43. Do you aspire to have *more money* than you can comfortably use?

44. Do you *talk about* your success to others, rather than letting your accomplishments speak for themselves?

45. Do you look for the seed of an equivalent benefit in all of your failures?

46. Are you guilty of *lazy thinking* about a main goal and how to obtain it?

47. Are you too quick to trust and too slow to verify?

48. Do you rage beyond mind control at un-solicited marketing calls?

49. Can you hold back *anger* when younger peers treat you as a child?

50. Do you *blow up* unnecessarily when family members try to make decisions for you?

APPENDIX 3b
INACCURATE THOUGHT PATTERNS
(Rule #2)

1. Needless worry and feelings of inferiority or being left out
2. Feelings that you can't surmount poverty and want
3. "Neuroticism" brought on by suspicions and unwanted fear
4. Allowing fear to bring about feelings of failure
5. Seeking something for nothing
6. Allowing others to control your mind
7. Dissatisfaction with (and griping about) one's work or situation
8. Doing no more than what you are paid for, or obligated for
9. Mourning over petty misfortunes
10. Expecting rewards and benefits prior to giving them out
11. Cultivating the negative emotions toward life and your fellow man
12. Encouraging indolence in charitable work
13. Making excuses for unfulfilled objectives

WRONGFUL THOUGHTS
(Rule #2)

HATRED	UNDEPENDABILITY	SLANDER
CRUELTY	HYPOCHRONDRIA	GOSSIP
IMPATIENCE	DECEIT	GREED
DISHONESTY	INDECISION	WORRY
DISLOYALTY	INJUSTICE	EGOTISM
INSINCERITY	ENVY	INTOLERANCE
FALSEHOOD	JEALOUSY	FEAR
MERCILESSNESS	LUST	REVENGE
OBSESSIVE VANITY	UNRIGHTEOUS ANGER	

LIFE'S TRUE REWARDS FOR SUCCESSFUL AGING
(Rule #12)

1. FREEDOM FROM FEAR
2. LOVE OF ONE'S WORK
3. HARMONY WITH OTHERS
4. DEFINITE FUTURE PLANS
5. GOOD HEALTH
6. ECONOMIC SECURITY
7. SHARING WITH OTHERS
8. CONTROL OF SELF
9. HOPE FOR THE FUTURE
10. POSITIVE ATTITUDE TOWARD LIFE
11. OPEN MIND
12. CONCERN FOR OTHERS

Appendix 3c
ESSENTIAL COMPONENTS OF LIFE — SEVEN POSITIVE AND NEGATIVE EMOTIONS

ESSENTIAL COMPONENTS FOR LIFE (RULE #4)

1. Physical concerns
2. Mental attitudes
3. Social involvements
4. Spiritual needs

THE SEVEN POSITIVE EMOTIONS (RULE #4)

1. Desire
2. Faith
3. Love
4. Sex
5. Enthusiasm
6. Romance
7. Hope

THE SEVEN NEGATIVE EMOTIONS (RULE #4)

1. Hate
2. Envy
3. Greed
4. Fear
5. Superstition
6. Revenge
7. Unrighteous Anger

Appendix 3d
STATEMENT OF GOALS
(Rule #4)

1. WRITE OUT A STATEMENT OF YOUR GOALS. This statement will be ineffective against criticism without these six little helpers: *"I had six honest serving men; they taught me all I knew. Their names were <u>What</u> and <u>Where</u> and <u>When</u> and <u>Why</u> and <u>How</u> and <u>Who</u>.* It is helpful to be specific in your wishes or prayers.

2. DEVELOP AN INTENSE ENTHUSIASM WITHIN YOURSELF OVER THE GOALS YOU'VE REACHED IN LIFE AND/OR YOUR PLANS TO ACHIEVE OTHER GOALS. You must act from the heart on this next point: Don't shut your doors against a setting sun. Unless you prefer the happiness of solitude, get yourself out of the old rocking chair and welcome the swinging days ahead. Spend less time searching for a shadow life in social media. Sing, dance, talk to yourself; practice, or volunteer your services, until you can feel the breath of achievement, and the fever of reason to utilize whatever talents God has given to you in life, and to enjoy moments of serenity for the gifts of goodness

you have passed on to others—this through your efforts and your very existence. Remember, criticism never opened a good show; nor closed down a bad one.

3. REPEAT THE STATEMENT OF GOALS NIGHT AND DAY AFTER EACH OF YOUR "ENTHUSIASM" OR "PRAYER" SESSIONS, BELIEVE THAT YOUR GOALS WILL BE ACTED UPON IN RETURN FOR SERVICES THAT YOU WILL GIVE, AND ARE GIVING TO OTHERS. EXPRESS GRATITUDE FOR WHAT IS YET TO COME. ASK AND YOU WILL RECEIVE.

To see yourself receiving rewards, and achieving and setting out goals, you must—through commensurate effort—promise and deliver something in return. The undying strength of this goal pact is your insurance against the undermining influence of criticism.

STATEMENT OF EXCHANGE
(See Rule #4)

In exchange for these rewards, I will perform to the best, highest, and fullest of my ability for the benefit of those receiving my services as (whatever your calling, position, or status in life). I believe that I will achieve these goals. Their accomplishment will come to me in proportion to my efforts expended to achieve these goals. I will recognize these opportunities when they are presented to me. And I will act on them when they are achieved. I accept the loan of thankfulness and all benefits given to me; and I will repay that loan by bringing happiness and humble service to others less fortunate than myself.

Appendix 3e
CONCENTRATION ESSENTIALS
(Rule #5)

1. **DEFINE AND PURSUE SPECIFIC GOALS**

   Most problems, well-organized and defined, are already partially solved. Move positively once your goals are clearly defined. i.e increased income; investments, cosmetic or other surgery; changes in habits, lifestyle, career; attitude; social expectations, diet; exercise; education; spirituality, etc.

2. **DEVELOP FAITH**

   Follow the precepts of the Nazarene who said, "Ask and it will be given to you; seek and you will find; knock and it will be opened to you. For everyone who asks, receives; and he who seeks, finds. *Matthew 7: 7-8*

"For truly I say to you, if you have faith as a grain of mustard seed, you will say to this mountain, (or obstacle) 'Move from here to there,' and it will move; and nothing will be impossible to you." *Matthew 17-20*

3. ADOPT A POSITIVE MENTAL ATTITUDE

Think success in achieving your goals! A greater part of our happiness or misery depends on our disposition and **not** on our circumstances. "I can't," is an idea—**not** a fact. Success is achieved and maintained by those who keep trying.

Appendix 3f
MASTER-MIND ALLIANCE DESCRIPTION
(Rule #6)

1. **The Guard of Mental Peace**

   Good Old Age brings us back with a fondness to all that is fresh in the early dawn of youth. Call on him to steer you away from taking illicit and questionable actions and to purge your mind of the seven negative emotions: Hate, Envy, Greed, Fear, Superstition, Revenge, and Anger.

2. **The Guard of Good Health**

   He who has health has hope, and he who has hope has everything. He protects one of life's great riches. Without this guard, you cannot effectively lead; for no person will long follow suffering and the specter of death.

3. **The Guard of Faith and Hope**

   Faith is the substance of things hoped for, the evidence of things not seen. He keeps the spiritual path open for you and shows you how—through *prayer* and *autosuggestion*— you can make direct and immediate contact with Infinite Intelligence. This guard shows you the way to a positive mental attitude.

4. **The Guard of Financial Success**

    This guard will offer you Aladdin's Lamp, aglow with ready money, wisdom, knowledge, and power. He keeps money worries away from you by "balancing your books." He is responsible for seeing that you give something of equal value for all monies received and expected.

5. **The Guard of Love**

    He who loves guards, is well guarded. He helps you to lead everyone you meet onto a higher plane than when you found them—to do unto others as you would have them do unto you. He makes you understand that you can never speak boldly of yourself without loss, for your accusations will always be believed, your praises never.

6. **The Guard of Wisdom**

    We become wiser by adversity, and often by age. This guard is responsible for the "mustering" of the other guards. His principal duty is to exchange failure and unpleasant circumstance for commensurate benefits. He reminds you that people relate themselves to one another in whatever jobs, capacities, or activities to which they are associated *because of a motive or motives*. Without this guard, you may forget that there can be no permanent human relationship based upon an indefinite or vague motive, or upon no motive at all. A widow or woman in retirement, for example, may be presumed by family and friends to be lonely and sad, when, in fact, she is happiest in the shadow of her work or manly loving heart—a clear motive for wanting to be alone and not a vagueness of cooperation with others.

Appendix 3g
Sample Mastermind Alliance

Sample "Master-Mind" Alliance

See RULE # 6 – Act to COOPERATE WITH OTHERS

William Shakespeare

Guard of Mental Peace

Ben Carson

Guard of Good Health

Billy Graham

Guard of Faith and Hope

Donald Trump

Guard of Financial Success

Mother Teresa

Guard of Love

Abraham Lincoln

Guard of Wisdom

Appendix 3h
KEY HUMAN MOTIVATIONAL POINTS
(Rule #7)

SELF-PRESERVATION

1. You are not entitled to live at the expense of others.

LIFE AFTER DEATH

2. Most of the world's religions believe in eternal life.

FREEDOM OF BODY AND MIND

3. These gifts are grants from the Creator.

SELF EXPRESSION

4. It is given to everyone; but not at the expense of harming others.

MATERIAL GAIN

5. Share with others what you have. That which remains multiplies and grows.

LOVE

6. Love is the greatest defense against the spears of hate and anger, and a skillful tool to open the hearts of others.

FEAR

7. Once overcome, fear will be turned into faith, and this assurance will return to you the possession of your mind, opening ways to grant your desires and reject any negative wishes.

SEXUALTY

8. The cup of sensual pleasure should never be drained to the bottom, for there is always poison in the dregs.

UNRIGHTEOUS ANGER

9. The fire you kindle for your enemy often burns yourself more than him.

HATE

10. Hatred is active, while envy is passive dislike. There is but one step from envy to hate.

Appendix 3i
HABITS for CREATING BRAIN POWER
(Rule #9)

1. Repeat to yourself that you are adopting those qualities of character and behavior patterns you find admirable in your imaginary cabinet. Many followers of Christ have achieved the dominant part of their character and behavior objectives through worship and prayer. Perform or pray this ritual daily until it becomes a habit.

   Words without thought, never to heaven go.
   — Shakespeare

2. Find opportunities to speak forcefully to others on topics of interest to them. Avoid controversy at this time.

3. Learn to control your nervous system and to become more agreeable. Avoid expressing your grievances and anger in front of others.

4. Remember the importance of your outward appearance. Your dress, as well as your behavior, is your table of contents.

5. Form the habit of making compliments from the heart.

6. Stick to your resolutions. Clear away half-finished tasks.

7. Devote your wholehearted effort to developing a positive attitude.

8. Remember that a personality change cannot be brought about overnight. Begin with small things, and build from there.

9. Recognize that because of the following inviolable rule, a pleasant personality can only come through practice: *Use breeds habit, and habit is stronger than nature.*

10. Don't be discouraged by occasional failures in your efforts to improve yourself. The expectations of life depend upon diligence; the mechanic who would perfect his work must first sharpen his tools.

11. Improve your memory with exercise. Physically able people who began to exercise in their 60's have reduced their risk of dementia by half.

12. Take up a new hobby such as music, painting, or foreign languages.

Appendix 3j
50 major failure habits
(Rule #11)

1. Lack of chief goals in life
2. Lack of self-confidence
3. Inability to take control of your own mind
4. Succumbing to any or all of the 7 basic fears
5. Accepting mediocrity as a standard
6. Procrastination
7. Lack of persistent endeavor
8. Lack of a positive mental attitude
9. Sour personality
10. Lack of gratitude for life's blessings
11. Expecting something for nothing
12. Inability to make decisions
13. Lack of personal knowledge and experience
14. Over-emphasis on formal learning
15. Unwillingness to take chances
16. Impatient attitude
17. Inability to accurately judge people

18. Lack of cooperative attitude
19. Over-emphasis on material concerns
20. Loss of harmony in marriage
21. Loss of spirituality
22. Inability to cultivate true friendships
23. Selfishness and greed
24. Uncontrolled envy
25. Lack of work effort
26. Indiscriminate spending
27. Dishonesty
28. Inaccurate thinking
29. Excessive ego
30. Lack of savings and capital
31. Intolerance
32. Abuse of power
33. Lack of enthusiasm
34. Lack of labor of love
35. Jack-of-all-trades syndrome
36. Excessive superstition and prejudice
37. Inability to discipline yourself
38. Lack of loyalty
39. Uncontrolled emotions

40. Lack of imagination

41. Inability to recognize opportunity

42. Unwillingness to do more than you're paid for

43. Vindictive attitude

44. Minding other peoples' business

45. Using vulgarity and slander

46. Lack of respect for constitutional authority

47. Unwillingness to accept advice and counsel

48. Carelessness in settling obligations to others

49. Drug use and alcoholism

50. Unjustified trust in people

Appendix 3k
EFFECTIVE LEADERSHIP QUALITIES
(Rule #12)

1. Freedom from fear
2. Control of self
3. Concern for others
4. Selflessness
5. Ability to delegate
6. Sense of justice
7. Accurate thought patterns
8. Tolerance and Patience
9. Temperance
10. Integrity
11. Ability to profit from failure
12. Courage to make decisions
13. Doing more than required
14. Attention to detail

15. Imaginative outlook
16. Willingness to be responsible
17. Humility
18. Team builder
19. Tactful personality
20. Concentration, persistence
21. Practice of the Golden Rule
22. Take the initiative
23. Acting with enthusiasm
24. Cooperate with others
25. Willingness to work, prepare
26. Definite goals and plans
27. Confidence in self
28. Ability to follow through
29. Dedication to duty
30. Respect for authority
31. Showmanship

TEN BASIC MOTIVES
(Rule #7)

1. Self-preservation
2. Life after death
3. Freedom of body and mind
4. Material gain
5. Recognition of self-expression
6. Emotion of love
7. Emotion of fear
8. Emotion of sex
9. Emotion of anger
10. Emotion of hate

Appendix 3L
HOW TO INFLUENCE THE SUBCONSCIOUS MIND
(Rule #13)

1. Write out a statement of your desires, such as a specific amount of money you will need to reach your level of comfort.

2. Determine in your statement exactly what services you intend to render in return for the money, such as vigorous and unremitting effort in some field of endeavor for your age and physical condition.

3. Establish a *definite* time frame and a specific date in your statement.

4. *Conceive* a workable plan for carrying out your desire, and *believe* you will soon achieve your goal(s) by implementing the plan whether it is completely ready or not. Express this belief in your statement.

5. Express *gratitude* in your statement for having been given the guidance necessary to carry out your plan.

6. Proceed with *enthusiasm,* and do not be dissuaded in your efforts to reach your goal. Affirm this in your statement.

7. Anticipate accomplishment of your goal by repeating in your statement that you will soon be in possession of the *specified* desires.

8. Read your written statement aloud—at least once in the morning and again at night—and, while reading, *see, feel,* and *believe* yourself in possession of your desires.

Lord, make me an instrument of your peace; where there is hatred, let me sow love; where there is injury, pardon; where there is doubt, faith; where there is despair, hope; where there is darkness, light; and where there is sad-ness, joy.
-St Francis

BACK OF THE BOOK

RELATED ITEMS FOR ALL AGES

Item #1—AGELESS THOUGHTS FROM THE GUARD OF WISDOM

Item #2—THE CHILLING POWER OF THE HUMAN MIND

Item #3—LOVE BOAT TO HEAVEN

Item #4—16 WAYS TO USE THE BIBLE IN YOUR PATH THROUGH LIFE

Item #5—LAUGHTER--- IT'S GOOD FOR YOU!

ITEM #1
AGELESS THOUGHTS FROM THE GUARD OF WISDOM

Just because two people argue, it doesn't mean they don't love each other, and just because they don't argue, it doesn't mean they do love each other.

We don't have to change friends if we understand that friends do change.

No matter how good a friend is, they're going to hurt you every once in a while, and you must forgive them for that.

True friendship continues to grow, even over the longest distance; same goes for true love.

You can do things in an instant that will give you a headache for life.

It's taking me a long time to be the person I want to be.

You should always leave loved ones with loving words. It may be the last time you see them.

You can keep going long after you think you can't.

We are responsible for what we do, no matter how we feel.

Either you control your attitude, or it controls you.

Heroes are the people who do what has to be done, when it needs to be done, regardless of the consequences.

Sometimes the people you expect to kick you when you're down are the ones who will help you to get back up.

Being angry does not give you the right to be cruel.

MORE AGELESS THOUGHTS FROM THE GUARD OF WISDOM

Maturity has more to do with what types of experiences you've had and what you're learned from them, and less to do with how many birthday's you've celebrated.

It isn't always enough to be forgiven by others. Sometimes you have to forgive yourself.

No matter how bad your heart is broken, the world doesn't stop for your grief.

Our background and circumstances may have influenced who we are; but we are responsible for who we become.

You shouldn't be so eager to find out a secret. It could change your life forever.

Two people can look at the exact same thing and see something totally different.

Your life can be changed in just hours by people who don't even know you.

SCRIPT AND FLAME

Even when you think you have no more to give, when a friend calls out for you – you will find the strength to help.

Those credentials on the wall do not make you a decent human being.

The people you care about most in life are taken from you too soon.

The happiest of people don't necessarily have the best of everything. They just make the most of what they have.

Inside every older person is a younger person wondering what the hell happened?

If you do not go after what you want, you'll never have it.

If you do not ASK, the answer will always be NO.

If you do not step forward, you'll always be in the same place.

ITEM #2
THE CHILLING POWER
OF THE HUMAN MIND

Can our minds act as a cog in an invisible wheel of life that can transfer thought into current reality through physically unknown, yet acknowledged mental channels of clairvoyance and telepathy? Memory and practice of the <u>16 Rules</u> in this healing book, *Script and Flame* can change your life in a positive way. When firmly embedded in your mind, these <u>16 proven rules</u> can magically make your future dreams come true. There is an invisible and undeniable force in the universe that—if tapped by the mind—can act effectively upon intense thoughts of good and evil. *I acknowledge that much of the literary substance, written words, and texture of this book were registered in time and transferred telepathically to my mind in response to my search for composition.* In simple words, *thoughts fly through time and space, landing on the wants of mankind.*

Clairvoyance is the supposed ability to perceive things that are not in sight or that cannot be seen, such as sending thoughts through time and space. *Telepathy* is the theory of causing someone to think or feel something by the use of one's mind, utilizing communication means beyond the standard physical senses—the process not to be confused with the abilities and practices of *psychics*.

Parapsychology is a professional term for practitioners addressing the mind facility of *extrasensory perception (ESP)*. All aspects of these, and similar "mind control" functions, are largely discredited by proponents of the *Bible* as "occult-like" practices.

With respect to Plato, Aristotle, all world religions, mystery theologians, spiritual universalists and believers in Masters of the Universe, etc. –and recognizing that the devil can quote scripture for his purpose—this discussion acknowledges divisiveness of subject matter. Opposition of viewpoints is also expected from religiosity cults whose extremists offer followers—among the lineage and liturgy of their prophets—(1) a hellish world of multiple virgins gifted to blood-thirsty men; (2) rousing physical rewards to apostates who kill disbelievers; (3) earthly promises of stoned and tormented women suffering in dust-filled streets; (4) the agonizing and tireless cacophony of tribal prayer calls; and (5) the rites of chopped heads from the necks of Judeo-Christians and "inhuman" outliers. It is also acknowledged by humans of whatever spiritual belief that there is an afterlife and that thought, feelings, and expectations are universal and projected outward.

It is natural as we age that many of our thoughts, in a material-measured world, would turn to spiritual issues. What lies beyond the confines of the earth? To a devout and God-fearing Christian, the answer to eternal celestial bliss is obviously to be embedded within the promise and realm of Heaven. The Holy Spirit has written the revelation of

God in the *Bible*; and his children of faith will all be coming home. The promises of Jesus are not open to question. *"The word of the Lord was growing mightily and prevailing."* (ACTS 19-20). Saint Thomas Aquinas bridged the gap between knowledge and belief. His thoughts of faith in God are considered sounder than science; and his philosophy is the official system of the most powerful church in Christendom.

In the *Bible*, we read of prophets who appear to have the ability to see into the future with precognition of time travel, though there is scarce evidence of any brain wave moving from one mind to another. The concept and thin reports of "thought transference" (telepathy) have been labeled—through scientific tests—as false and anecdotal; however, in this computer age, the idea of *"Quantum Mechanics"* has gained some mental traction within the bounds of scientific theory, and through the reintroduction of telepathy as a possible spiritual channel of communication.

Chrystalinks.com reports an assertion from proponents of "thought transference" that *"telepathy is not "extrasensory" – rather (1) that the brain is the telepathic organ in the thought process; (2) that its connection from one mind to another brain is not physical, but psychic; and (3) that the very definition of the psychic medium is the "localized inertial frame of reference which is affected by the mind."*

SCRIPT AND FLAME

<u>In plain down-to-earth talk, the theory of *thought transfer* over time and space is claimed by some scientific investigators to be possible, as new discoveries are unearthed in studies of the brain.</u>

In direct or idle opposition to the Maker's invisible wall of protection for the human mind from random hordes of invading, indiscriminant, and wandering thoughts, it is theoretically and respectfully conceivable that an "iron web" of thought patterns exists in the unseen world that can be penetrated or abridged by forces of human mind control—both good and evil in nature—and within the objective mode. Minimally invasive and unconscious "Google-like" mental searches by people seeking human attributes of material, emotional, and health concern can be helped or misguided in their quest for satisfaction or information, *since their search could act as either a beneficent result or solution, or as a deadly mental disease that can spread over time into a ruminant infection of good or evil in the achievement of want, need, desire, and goals in life.*

Understand that this discussion is beyond the frequency of the 5 physical senses – sight, hearing, touch, taste and smell, and doesn't demean or disparage the use of prayer as rightful communication with God.

"We look <u>*not*</u> at the things that are seen, but at the things which are <u>*not*</u> seen: for the things which are <u>*not*</u> seen are eternal." 2 COR. 4:18.

Telepathic communication can be reflected in dreams that are moving faster than the speed of light. Examples of these phenomena are beyond speech and body language and are perceptible in the time-worn elements of love, sexual needs, and innate family concerns. In addition to telepathy, other paranormal forms of extra-sensory perception, such as clairvoyance and parapsychology, are reflected in the ageless *Bible,* and are—in tune with *Biblical* culture—characterized as a form of witchcraft infested with daemons—not unlike the realms of abominable dictators and tyrants of today who seek to channel unclean spirits and perpetuate evil and occultist thoughts to control the minds of God's children on earth. *Then the magicians, the enchanters, the Chaldeans, and the astrologers came in, and I told them the dream; but they could not make known to me its interpretation.* Daniel 4: 7

Shakespeare said that it is the mind that makes the body rich, and *Emerson* said that each mind has its own method. *Cicero* said that the diseases of the mind are more and more destructive than those of the body. The *Bible* says, *"In the beginning was the Word, and the word was with God, and the word was God."* John 1:1 – and...

"Beware of practicing your righteousness among other people to be seen by them, for you will have no reward from your Father who is in Heaven. Thus, when you give to the needy, sound no trumpet. . .do not let your left hand know what your right hand is doing. . .and when you pray, you must not be like the hypocrites. . .Truly I say to you, they

have received their reward." Matthew 6: 1- 34

REMEMBER! YOU MUST NOT CONFLATE PRAYER WITH MIND CONTROL

Prayer, of course, is a gift of God. Discipline of the mind is the object of mind control. True prayers should come from the heart—not asking for too much for anyone or anything, thus causing prayer failure.

TRUE STORY – <u>One thought cannot awake without waking others.</u>

Theorists on death and aging suggest that the soul never dies and that heretical characteristics transfer through dead bodies to the eternal souls of the newly born, injecting a legacy of attributes that can advance or hinder human progress on earth. Psychics, hypnotists, metaphysical gurus, and *Biblical* scholars recount the existence of clairvoyance and telepathy and the influence of these spiritual channels of communication in matters of the mind. The tale begins at my chimney corner.

The story whirls around like a potter's wheel, past talk of ancestral legacies to the theoretical transfer of thoughts into actions through the ages, stopping at the period 1734-38 at the limited reign of a German immigrant named Hans Jost Heydt, aka Jost Hite, who purchased a land grant and helped to colonize a country-sized wilderness. Hite was a strong leader and adventuresome land developer—one of the first settlers in the Shenandoah Valley. His son, Isaac—

> Major Hite in the Revolutionary War—was an aide to General Muhlenberg and the builder of my historic home and homestead, known in the pages of yesteryear as "The Forest."

B.K. Haynes is a renowned land developer who—it can be telepathically argued—took up the torch of Jost Hite's career in the Shenandoah Valley and developed more than 300 square miles of land over four highly populated states—a territory that extends from the Eastern Seaboard to the highest mountain peaks east of the Mississippi River, while developing and selling off many parcels he called "Land Grants"—exactly the terminology of Jost Hite's purchase. And for almost half a century B.K. Haynes has lived in the home originally built by Jost Hite's son.

Hite's son, Isaac, was a man of strong character who has no ancestral or informative past connection with Haynes—*only a noted spiritual link, somewhere in time, through the chilling power of the human mind.*

I was unaware at the time I purchased my farm that the act of owning this particular farm may have been an instrument of Heaven, playing to my desires, and not a surrender to mystical "oneness" theories of mankind, where *everything* belongs to *everybody*—each branded with a destiny to follow specified visionary and idealistic paths in life. What supernatural creator, or clairvoyant and telepathic power, determines the fate and future of each human being? How can we control our circumstances and enjoy our lives on earth if everything is done by immutable laws, and if our destiny is already recorded in celestial files? Of course, life is a diverse and long winding road for each of us to travel—the path through our unseen and final days on earth shaped by the robbing troops of circumstance. Confucius said that only life and death have determined appointments on this challenging roadway, and that honor depends on Heaven. So a life well spent—with cognition and practice of *Biblical* Rules can therefore induce varied degrees of happiness and success within a person's calling and persona—the degree depending on the strength of the seeker's determination to succeed and move forward in life. Winged thoughts tend—over the horizon of time—to flock with birds of the same feather.

TRUE STORY – *One thought cannot awake without waking others.*

B.K. Haynes began writing his first novel, *The idealESTATE MAN,* while on a trip around the world. In the Australian Outback, he felt sufficiently cut loose from business ties in the U.S. to begin unfolding an incredible tale of self-destruction that, in a bizarre way, transmuted shortly thereafter into actual occurrences in real life. Research for the book took him to storied centers of intrigue and adventure, such as Singapore, Caracas, San Francisco, the Bahamas and Lake Tahoe in the High Sierras.

B.K. HAYNES

In 1977, B.K. Haynes writes in his story about a young developer who blows up a casino in northern Nevada. B.K. Haynes details the evacuation drama. In 1977—before the Haynes book is published—bombs are planted in a northern Nevada casino.

Under a clever management ruse, meant to keep the bomb threat a secret, everyone is evacuated. Get this! <u>The bomb plant, the threat, the evacuation, everything is the same as written—except the actual explosion and fire.</u>

B.K. Haynes writes in *The idealESTATE MAN* of a misguided band of idealists from the West Coast who wage a campaign of violence against the establishment and its doctrine that comfort, wealth, and pleasure are the only and highest human values. <u>In 1977—after the book was written—before publication of the book—a terrorist group in San Francisco waged an eight-day campaign against the rich and claimed responsibility for four bomb attacks aimed at San Francisco wealth.</u>

B.K. Haynes writes in his book about a young idealist man who flees his family and materialistic life in an attempt to "disappear" from the face of the earth. He goes underground and falls in love with a young woman who shares his beliefs; and she helps him hide from the police. <u>In 1977—after the book was written—a young man in the same West Coast area, left his family, vowing never to return to the "status-seeking" life he had known. He faked death and fled to the mountains with a young woman who shared his beliefs; and she helped him hide from the police.</u>

SCRIPT AND FLAME

In 1978, before *The idealESTATE MAN* is published, the Rev. Jim Jones writes from his suicidal religious settlement in Guyana about a real-life scene he had witnessed. <u>This scene is an uncanny re-enactment of a scene in the Haynes book!</u>

B.K. Haynes writes in *The idealESTATE MAN* about a bizarre narcotics smuggling operation in which an outdated intercontinental seaplane is utilized. In 1976—after Haynes had written it—<u>a similar scheme came to the attention of narcotics agents in Washington D.C. You guessed it. A prop-driven intercontinental seaplane was involved in the episode.</u>

B.K. Haynes writes in *The idealESTATE MAN* about an ailing recluse and casino owner who dies under mysterious circumstances after a jet aircraft had been sent to remove him to the hospital. <u>In 1976—again after Haynes had written it—an ailing Howard Hughes, also a noted casino owner dies in flight, en route to a hospital.</u>

Following the flight path of wandering thoughts through time, we find Howard Hughes—a villainous billionaire in the Haynes book—transfigured into a mysterious character, played by movie star Warren Beatty in his 2016 film, *Rules Don't Apply*. Haynes, with no ancestral, personal, or professional connection with Beatty, has owned the home and maintained offices in the Beaty House in Front Royal, VA for almost 50 years—a home where Beatty spent a measure of his childhood visiting relatives.

My book, *Racing Past 80* and the Beatty film both first appeared for public view in the year 2016. Is this sequence of events coincidence, or the consolidation of telepathic visitations by winged thoughts, landing again in the mind of B.K. Haynes almost three centuries from their origination at the Hite farm in Virginia? Strange indeed. B.K. Haynes writes below:

In writing this book I feel as if I had tuned in a "thought" channel of sorts, where relative material—and even drama—were filtered down to me from some unseen source. For example, my favorite actress from my teen years, Debbie Reynolds, died at the conclusion of my book. She was once married to my favorite singer in those days, Eddie Fisher. I was also influenced by the dynamic film, *Elmer Gantry*, with its multiple heart-driven messages from the word of God contained in the *Bible*. I concluded that I was simply a messenger for a great portion of my book, particularly in the aspect of soul-searching, determining God's will for those on earth, and separating life's saints from its scoundrels—where you reap what you sow. Now I know I am leaving a dark forest and on a *Yellow Brick Road* through ageless years.

B.K. Haynes—a writer and student of the human mind and world religions—was born January 13, 1934 in Laurel, Maryland. His mother and father were God-gifted, yet unproductive writers; his grandfather was a businessman, editor, and chief of publications in the Agriculture Department under Henry Wallace, who was later Chief of the Commerce Department and VP in the Roosevelt administration, when a quarter of the American people still lived on farms. Wallace introduced food stamps, and subsistence plans for farmers to curtail rural poverty. <u>Similar to B.K. Haynes, Wallace, in his early years, *explored spiritualism and became a scholar of esoteric religion* and was often called a mystic. B.K. Haynes— a follower of Jesus, and an evangelical; and like Wallace, also emerged in agricultural pursuits</u>—writes from his historic cattle farm in the fabled Shenandoah Valley of Virginia and is still active in land brokerage and development, and in issues related to the assistance, health, and well being of those entering the last cycle of life before leaving the earth.

ITEM #3
THE LOVE BOAT TO HEAVEN FROM THE SCHOOL OF LOVE

The kingdom of Heaven is likened to a treasure hidden in a field. Which a man having found, hid it, and for joy thereof goeth, and selleth all that he hath, and buyeth that field. Again, the kingdom of Heaven is like to a merchant seeking good pearls. Who, when he had found one pearl of great price, went his way, and sold all that he had, and bought it.

Of course, this does not mean that love leads inevitably to poverty. Sometimes it does; sometimes it demands a surrender even of the things of earth. A millionaire can love as well as a pauper; where love leads, a pauper can give as much as a millionaire. *For it is the gift of oneself that matters; the gift of a human heart; its homage; its reverence; its service. Those who serve, also serve those who only stand and wait.* "Christ loved me, and gave himself to me," said St. Paul. But undoubtedly it will be something that you will not be consulted as to what it shall be.

Be led by something more than mere argument, or reasoning of your own, that dead and fallacious thing that is the offspring of man's short sight; see without turning aside, submit to, without drawing back; be guided without flinching, to the compelling truth in itself; of nobility in itself; of beauty; of goodness; wherever these may be found. And lastly, when the spirit is moved to act, to give itself for something noble, to follow the light, to do that which is, in itself, worth doing; then let it go.

When you have made a certain way, and you have laughed and sung along the road, then love will begin to lead you through darker ways, where you did not want to go; it will ask you surrenders for which you had not bargained. It will disappoint you; it will fail to recognize you, it will leave your noblest actions unfulfilled, the noblest of your powers of your soul undeveloped. It will misinterpret your best motives; will envy your worthiest deeds; will crush you with sarcasm; will embitter you with mistrust, suspicion, dislike, and contempt. At critical moments, it will turn its back on you, will ignore your pleas when you are down. It will see you wounded on the road and pass you by; crucified, and say it was only your desert when you're down.

And then, when it has killed you, you will come to know. "He that loses his life for my sake shall find it." When it has purified you, when there is not left a spark of that mean thing called "self," when you no longer look for relief, for consolation, for comfort; but only for strength to go on, then will come the revelation. Then you will know that which, by any other training eye, can never see, nor hear; nor can it enter into the heart of man to conceive.

"Love is patient, is kind. Love envieth not, dealeth not perversely; is not puffed up, is not ambitious, seeketh not her own, is not provoked to anger, thinketh no evil, rejoiceth not in iniquity, but rejoiceth with the truth; heareth all things. Love never falleth away... Follow after love." (I Corinthians 13: 4-8)

ENEMIES OF LOVE

(1) Unrighteous Anger

(2) Impatience

(3) Envy

(4) Ego

(5) Greed

(6) Wickedness

(7) Unjustness

(8) Dishonesty

(9) Imprudence

(10) Disparity

(11) Fear

ITEM #4
16 WAYS TO USE THE BIBLE IN YOUR PATH THROUGH LIFE

1. ## When in sorrow

   <u>Read John 14</u>: Jesus said, "I am the way, the truth, and the light. No one comes to the Father except through me..."

2. ## When men fail you

   <u>Read Psalm 27</u>: When my father and my mother forsake me, then the Lord will take care of me.

3. ## When you have sinned

   <u>Read Psalm 51</u>: Wash me thoroughly from my iniquity and cleanse me from sin.

4. ## When you worry

   <u>Read Matthew 6:19-34</u>: ..."Therefore do not worry, saying, "What shall we eat, or what shall we drink, or wear." For your heavenly Father knows that you need all these things. But seek first the kingdom of God and his righteousness...

5. ## When you are in danger

   <u>Read Psalm 91</u>: I will say to the Lord, "He is my refuge and my fortress; My God, in Him I will trust...

6. You have the blues

    <u>Read Psalm 34</u>: The eyes of the Lord are on the righteous, and His ears are open to their cry. .

7. When God seems far away

    <u>Read Psalm 139</u>: O, LORD, you have searched me and known me. You know my sitting down and my rising up; You understand my thoughts afar off.

8. When you are discouraged

    <u>Read Isaiah 40</u>: Those who wait on the LORD shall renew their strength; They shall mount up with wings like eagles, They shall not be weary. . .

9. If you feel down and out

    <u>Read Psalm 23</u>: The Lord is my shepherd; I shall not want. He maketh me lie down in green pastures; He leads me beside the still waters. He restores my soul.

10. If you want courage for your task

    <u>Read Joshua 1</u>: "No man shall be able to stand before you all the days of your life, as I was with Moses; so I will be with you. I will not leave you nor forsake you."

11. When the world seems bigger than God

<u>Read Psalm 90</u>: Lord, You have been our dwelling place for generations . . .the days of our lives are 70 years; and by reason of strength they are eighty years. . .

12. When you want rest and peace

<u>Read Matthew 11:25-30</u>: "Come to me all you who labor and are heavy laden, and I will give you rest. . . for my yoke is easy and My burden is light. . .

13. When leaving home for labor and travel <u>*Read Psalm 121   107:23-31*</u>: I will lift my eyes to the hills—From whence cometh my help? My help comes from the LORD, Who made Heaven and earth. . . The Lord shall preserve your going out and your coming in, from this time forth and even for evermore. . . Those who go down to the sea in ships, who do business on great waters. . .they see his wonders. . .For He commands and raises the stormy winds, Which lifts up waves of the sea. . .He turns rivers into a wilderness. . .He turns wilderness into pools of water. . .He pours contempt on princes, and causes them to wander in the wilderness when there is no way. Yet He sets the poor on high, far from affliction . . .Whoever is wise will observe these things, and they will understand the loving kindness of the LORD.

14. **If you get bitter or critical**

   Read 1st Corinthians 13: Though I speak with the tongues of men and of angels, but have no love, I have become sounding brass or a clanging cymbal. And though I have the gift of prophesy and understand all mysteries and all knowledge, and though I have all faith, so I could move mountains, but have not love, I am nothing. And though I bestow all my goods to feed the poor, and though I give my body to be burned, but have not love, it profits me nothing ...

15. **If thinking of investments and returns**

   Read Mark 10:17-31: Jesus said, "it is easier for a camel to go through the eye of a needle than for a rich man to enter the kingdom of God. . . assuredly I say to you, there is no one who has left house of brothers or sisters, or father or mother, or wife and children, or lands, for My sake and the gospel's, who shall not receive a hundredfold now in this time—houses and brothers and sisters and mothers and children and lands, with persecutions—and in the age to come, eternal life. But many who are first will be last, and the last first."

16. ## For a great invitation – a great opportunity

    Read Isaiah 55: Seek the LORD while he may be found. Call upon him when he is near. Let the wicked forsake his way, and the unrighteous man his thoughts; Let him return to the LORD, and He will have mercy on him; and to our God, for He will abundantly pardon, for "My thoughts are not your thoughts; nor are your ways my ways," says the LORD."

    SUBMITTED WITH REVERENCE BY JAY AHLEMANN, PASTOR

    RESTORATION FELLOWSHIP CHURCH

ITEM #5
LAUGHTER—IT'S GOOD FOR YOU!
LOUISE KRESS CLARK

Laughter is important in our lives and especially more so as we face the problems that our aging and senior years bring our way!

"Those who can laugh never grow old." So let's learn to laugh!

Laughter helps keep us youthful and improves our thinking processes. It is good for our heart and our mind. The act of laughing stimulates the production of endorphins and helps you feel good instantly. Endorphins are the body's natural opiates, designed to relieve stress and enhance pleasure and feelings of happiness and euphoria. Laughter is like good medicine — and It's FREE! Laughter has many other physical and emotional benefits, and it seems to improve your disposition! Laughter helps to relieve stress which is known to cause all sorts of problems in our mind and body. Stress can also affect our memory—so we need to keep laughter in our lives.

We can find humor in everyday events—in fashion, in some types of music, in holidays (such as Halloween and April Fool's Day) in the comic strips of newspapers, in books of humor, and in magazines such as *Reader's Digest*. We even find humor in the bloops made by newscasters regarding current events. Look for humor and share it with others! Share a funny episode from a movie or television show, or share a funny story or joke of your own. Make a habit to spend more time around funny people! The more we laugh—the better we feel. We can laugh with others—and/or we can laugh alone.

Laughter can help make our lives happier. As we age, we need to feel good about ourselves. We are still capable of enjoying life, and also possibly falling in love. Be open to love! Have more sex. Having sex will boost your happiness right away. Being intimate with someone releases endorphins that make you feel great. You have the combined feeling of love, plus the benefits of physical touch. The feeling you get when a loved one walks into a room is the result of a mini flood of endorphins. Adding more love to your life is a great way to improve your happiness level. This is true of both romantic love, and of platonic love (*such as love for a friend, or pet*).

There is no limit to how happy you can be. Be good to yourself. Accept yourself and love yourself just the way you are—even as we advance through the Good Old Age! (GOA)

Speaking of age—at what age do we become old? When we were teenagers, fifty-five seemed really OLD; but by the time we reached fifty-five it didn't seem old anymore. We still felt YOUNG. Someone who is sixty-five refers to the forty-five year olds as young folks, and an eighty year oldster will say the sixty-five year old is still young. It seems that OLD AGE CHANGES AS A PERSON AGES.

The other day I read—"*You know you're getting old when you know your way around but you no longer care about going.*" It's also said that age is a state of mind—that you're only as old as you feel. If that's the case, it means that sometimes I'm young, sometimes I'm old; and sometimes I'm somewhere in the middle. Think young—and keep laughing. So here goes a laugh or two!

Three retirees—each with a hearing loss—were playing golf one fine spring day. One man remarked to the others "*windy, isn't it?*" "*No*", the second man replied, "*it's Thursday*" and the third man chimed in with "*I'm thirsty too. Let's go have a beer!*"

Two elderly ladies had been friends for many decades. Over the years they had shared all kinds of activities and adventures. Lately their activities had been limited to meeting a few times a week to play cards. One day they were playing cards when one looked at the other and said, "*Now don't get mad at me*—I know we've been friends for a long time, but I just can't think of your name! *Please tell me what your name is.*" Her friend glared at her for at least three minutes and then said, "*How soon do you need to know?*"

The minister was preparing his sermon and his little daughter was watching him. "*Daddy,*" she asked, "*does God tell you what to say?*" "*Of course*" the father answered. "*Why do you ask?*" "*Oh*" said the little girl, "*Then why do you scratch some of it out?*"

Did you hear about the man who sat up all night wondering where the sun went? *It finally dawned on him*!

Laughter is contagious! Make yourself and others happy with Laughter! Keep Laughing and Smiling!

Index

A

Abysmal Failure, 38, 39
accomplishment, 13, 38, 42, 73, 101, 149, 151, 161, 174, 219, 237
accurate thought, 23, 31, 194, 197
action, xviii, 11, 46, 65, 95, 98, 133, 148, 152, 154, 159, 165, 169, 194, 195
ADMIT, 38, 40, 41, 125
adversity, 43, 47, 65, 86, 223, 281
advice and counsel, 132, 232
agers, xviii, 54, 57, 80, 109, 153, 172, 189, 281
agnostics, 174
Ahlemann, Jay, 4, 263
Aladdin's lamp, 71, 203
Alda, Alan, 192
al-Assad, Dr., 183, 184
al-Assad, Khaled, 183, 184
Allies, 82
Alzheimer's, 62, 76, 97, 111
Ambruzzo, 126
American Indian, 59
Anderson, 126
Angela's Ashes, 190
Anger, 6, 63, 64, 85, 89, 92, 93, 213, 222, 227, 258
Apostle Peter, 129
Aquinas, Saint Thomas, 246
Arab proverb, 167
Aristotle, 112, 245
arrogance, 62
atheists, 174
Atlantic City, 33
ATM, 67
Augustine, 141

autosuggestion, 85, 112, 133, 154, 170, 222, *See* self-hypnosis
Axis Power, 82

B

Babylonian, 15
balloonists, 126, 127
basic motives, 90
Beaty House, 253
Beatty, Warren, 253, 254
Beethoven, 191
belief, 13, 41, 42, 59, 100, 148, 149, 154, 169, 170, 171, 172, 173, 174, 236, 245, 246
Berlin, Irving, 96
Bettger, Frank, 170
Bible, 9, 10, 52, 54, 82, 100, 105, 174, 192, 204, 245, 246, 248, 254
Biblical, 10, 11, 129, 174, 248, 249, 251
Branson, Missouri, 47
Brain Power, 207
bravery, 177
Broadway musicals, 99
Buddy, 18
Buffett, Warren, 83, 108, 142
Burroughs, 112

C

cabinet, 16, 85, 98, 106, 107, 109, 112, 116, 228
caliphates, 118
Camelot, 5
Camp Lejeune, xiv

Capuchin Seminary, xiv
Carnegie, Andrew 73, 83, 110, 111, 119, 142, 155, 156, 277
Carnegie, Dale, 110. 119
Cash Flow, 47,48
Catholics, 183
Central Intelligence Agency, xiv
Change, 5, 23, 26, 37, 55, 77, 103, 110-111, 139, 167, 174, 192, 229, 240, 242, 244
Chesapeake Bay, 30
chief goal in life, 140, 147
Christ, 54, 89, 90, 99, 103, 108, 112, 118, 129, 142, 173, 228, 256
Christian liturgy, 53
Christianity, 174
Churchill, Winston, 44, 108
Cicero, Marcus Tullius, 180, 248
Church of England, 184
Churchill, 189
Clairvoyance, 9, 244, 248, 249
Clark, Louise Kress, 264
Clark, Roy, 75
Collier, Robert, 151
Colonel Harlan Sanders, See Sanders, Colonel Harlen
Colton, Arthur, 16
Compassion, 80
concentrate, 41, 51, 75, 76, 171
concentration, v, 52, 73-78, 146, 155, 159, 198, 234
confidence, 3, 37, 38, 39, 40, 41, 44, 58, 74, 108, 110, 112, 130, 230
Copperfield, David,191
constitutional authority, 132, 232
conviction, 69, 172
counselors, 80
creativity, 47, 189
Creator, 39, 60, 70, 89, 92, 160, 170, 226
CREATORS, 189, 276
criminal activity, 46, 165
Criticism, 66, 67, 154

Cruelty, 115

D

D.C. Department of Recreation, 3
Danforth, William, 100, 278
Davis, Bette, 179
Day, Doris, 189
defeat, 5, 28, 47, 53, 79, 82, 97, 100, 124, 125, 128, 130, 163, 197, 210
Defense Investigative Service, xiv
definite chief aim, 150, 156, 174, 175
Definite Goals, 42
dementia, 62, 104, 114, 229
Denmark, 35
Depression of 1929, 15
desire, xi, 13, 46, 63, 64, 65, 69, 87, 100, 111, 136, 143, 147, 149, 151, 152, 153, 154, 169, 173, 174, 190, 204, 215, 236, 247
despots, 61, 76
Dickens, Charles, 191
DiMaggio, Joe 38
DiMaggio's, 75
disbelief, 68, 90, 154
disbelievers, 174, 245
discipline, 59, 103, 127, 132, 170, 177, 231
Discover Card, 30
disharmony, 46, 165
dishonesty, 132, 232, 258
distress, 68, 80
Double Eagle II, 126
Dowell, Jeanne, 190
Dr. Jekyll and Mr. Hyde, 191

E

Edison, Thomas, 74
ego, 38,42,44,51,87,110,135
Eisenhower, 82, 116, 138
elder, 45, 58, 81
elders, xviii, 50, 67, 79, 80, 104,

122, 153, 179, 182, 279, 281
election; 2016 Presidential election, 35
Elmer Gantry, 254
Elysian Fields, 54
Emerson, Ralph Waldo, 105, 128, 148, 160, 166,199, 248
Emerson's Essay on Compensation, 166
EMOTION OF ANGER, 89
EMOTION OF FEAR, 89
EMOTION OF HATE, 89
EMOTION OF LOVE, 89
EMOTION OF SEX, 89
enthusiasm, 13, 42, 63, 64,132, 137, 146, 149, 160, 169, 170, 171, 172, 173, 174, 175, 215, 231, 234, 237
Environmentalists, 48
Envy, 63, 64, 85, 216, 222, 258
Epictetus, 58
Esper, Fr. Joseph, 129
eternity, 13, 50, 54, 142
Eudaimonia. Hedonism, 151
Eudora Welty, 184
Europe, 82
Evangelists, 44
Excessive ego, 132, 231
extra mile, 163, 164, 166, 167

F

Fall, Alfred, 16
Failure, 76, 124, 126, 136, 170, 199
Failure Habits, 130
faith, 6, 39, 40, 47, 52, 54, 55, 63, 64, 77, 85, 93, 108, 110, 138, 160, 167, 170, 171, 172, 174, 177, 184, 191, 204, , 215, 221, 222, 227, 246, 262
Father Forgets, 119
Fear, 39, 53, 55, 57, 59, 63, 64, 66, 68, 85, 89, 213, 216, 222, 227, 258

fears and emotions, 50
financial sages, 45
Financial Success, 108, 223
Fisher, Eddie, 254
Fitzgerald, F. Scott, 141
Flame, i, 9, 10, 11, 12, 41, 98, 140, 197, 280
fool, 166, 167
Ford, Henry, 73, 84, 100
forgiveness, 167
formal learning, 131, 230
Fort Myer, 3
Franklin, Benjamin, 170, 176, 190
FREEDOM OF BODY AND MIND, 89, 92, 226
Frenchmen, 126
friendships, vii, xv, 80, 82, 130, 131, 231
Front Royal, xi, 253

G

Gandhi, Mahatma, 108
Gary Cooper, 38
Gates, Bill, 83, 142
General Electric, 4
George Washington University, 3, 18
Getty, John Paul, 135
Gladstone, 189
Glenn, John, 178
goal pact, 70, 218
goals, 10, 12, 23, 31, 42, 68, 70, 76-78, 101, 112, 147, 150-161, 170, 173, 176, 198, 199, 203, 207, 209, 217-221, 247
God, xvii, 7, 10, 23, 28, 40, 41, 44, 51, 53, 54, 56, 61, 68, 70, 81, 91, 99, 107, 117, 120, 138, 142, 153, 157, 174, 189, 191, 192, 209, 217, 245, 247, 248, 249, 254, 255, 259, 260, 261, 262, 263, 266
Golden Rule, 89, 91, 146, 234
good character, 112, 114, 203

good old age, 56, 67, 69, 98, 179, 189, 200, 222, 265, 280
Good Samarian, 106
Graham, Billy, 96, 108
Grandma Moses, 96
gratitude, 28, 131, 149, 209, 230, 237
greed, 52, 63, 64, 85, 96, 131, 216, 222, 258
Guard of Financial Success, The, 86
Guard of Love, The, 86
Guard of Mental Peace, The, 85
Guinness Book of Records, 74

H

H. W. Shaw, 189
habits, 7, 13, 25, 28, 77, 89, 112, 129, 133, 134, 136, 140, 209, 220, 280
Hagerty, Barbara Bradley, 104, 278
harmony in marriage, 131, 231
Hayes, Helen, 96
Haynes, Bradley K., xv, 278
Harry S. Truman, 140
Harvard study, 56
Hate, 63, 64, 85, 89, 216, 222
Hawaii, 6, 99
Hawthorne, 195
Heaven, 7, 53, 54, 68, 80, 86, 96, 104, 108, 118, 148, 174, 245, 248, 250, 256, 261
hedonism, 151
Hemmingway, Ernest, 141
Hereford, 183
Herrod, 12
Hessian Soldier, 4
Heydt, Hans Jost, 249
High Noon, 38
Hillary, Sir Edmund, 83
Hitler, Adolf, 9, 76, 117
Hitler's 3rd Reich, 9
Hobson, Howard, 16
Holiday Inns, 84

hope, 6, 26, 39, 55, 63, 64, 83, 85, 108, 124, 129, 141, 144, 148, 149, 181, 190, 215, 222
Hope, 55, 85, 222
How to Win Friends and Influence People, 110, 119
Hughes, Howard, 283
human abuse, 46
Human Mind, the, 42, 90, 117, 172, 194, 247, 250, 255
hypnotists, 170
hypochondria, 57

I

I = Can, 42
I Dare You, 100
IdealEstate Man, 251, 252, 253
idealism, 47
imaginary advisors, 108
Imagination, 95, 100
imagined obstacles, 49
Impatient attitude, 131, 230
inaccurate thinking, 30, 49, 132, 231
inaccurate thought patterns, 22, 197
India, 142
Indiscriminate spending, 132, 231
Infinite Intelligence, 39, 40, 41, 42, 86, 223
initiative, 12, 108, 138, 139, 140, 143, 146, 199, 234
Iraqi Republican Guard in 2003, 138

J

Jack-of-all-trades, 132, 231
Japanese, 99
Jefferson, 103
Jesse Owens, 108
Jesus, 23, 61, 89, 90, 99, 103, 110, 117, 118, 129, 173, 174, 246, 255, 259, 262
Jew, 118

Jimmy Stewart, xiii
Job's wonder, 64
Jobs, 82, 83, 86, 223
Jobs, Steve, 108, 142
Johns Hopkins University, xiv
judgment, 41, 49, 135, 172

K

Kauffman Foundation, 190
Kemble, St. John, 183
Kennedy, John F., 5
Kenny, Sister Elizabeth, 191
Kentucky Fried Chicken, 190
Kidnapped, 191
King, Martin Luther, 108, 118
Knight, Bobby, 75
Kruger, Ivor, 16

L

land boom, 5, 280
Lansbury, Angela, 192
Laws of Success, 150, 175
Lazarus, 6
Leadership, 3, 138
Leadership School, 3
Leadership Qualities, 139
Life After Death, 89, 92, 226, 277
life's blessings, 131, 230
Lincoln, 103, 108, 116, 126
Lindberg, 38
Livermore, Jesse, 16
Larned, W. Livingston, 119
London Sunday Times, 84
LONELINESS, 61
Longfellow, 176
Lorayne, Harry, 170
Lord of Learning, 129
lost love, 61, 63
love, 7, 32, 44, 56, 61, 62, 63,
    64,75, 89,93, 108, 120, 121,
    132, 144,147, 150, 151,
    154,155, 167, 174, 176, 181,
    182, 191, 193, 204, 215, 223,
227, 231, 235, 240, 248, 252,
    256, 257, 258, 262, 265
loyalty, 132, 231

M

MacArthur, General, 99, 100, 138
Mandino, Og, 12
Manhattan, 32, 34
Manifesto of Travel, 7
Marshall, General George C., 82, 138
MasterCard, 30
Master of Ballantrae, the, 191
Mastermind, 84
Material Gain, 89, 93, 226
Mattis, General James "Mad Dog" 138
Mayo Clinic, 104
McCourt, Frank, 190
mediocrity, 131, 230
meditation, 59
melancholia, 62
memory, 7, 11, 67, 76, 104, 111,
    114, 122, 161, 187, 198, 229,
    264, 281
Mental Attitude, 42, 63, 215
Mental Peace, 108, 222
metaphysical gurus, 249
metaphysical thoughts, 58
Miserey, 126
missionaries, 81
moral desires, 152
Moral High Ground, 91
morality, 90
Moses, 178, 260
Moses, Robert, 32
Mother Teresa, 108
Muhlenberg, General, 252
murder, 62

N

nagging, 68
name calling, 67

Nancy, 83
Napoleon Hill, 11, 40, 57, 73, 83, 108, 109, 150, 172, 175, 277
narcissism, 62
National Rifle Association, xv
nationalism, 118
Natural Forces, 10
nature, 9, 53, 59, 60, 62, 65, 66, 101, 109, 114, 124, 128, 142, 152, 153, 161, 165, 166, 199, 229, 247
Naval Investigative Service, xiv
Nazarene, 77, 220
NCIS, x, xiv
negative attitudes, 21
Neurochemical, 116
New Age apostates, 54
Newman, 126
Newton, Sir Isaac, 76
New York City, 32, 33, 34, 116
Nightingale, Florence, 192
Nineteen Stars, 138
North Africa, 82

O

O'Brian, M.D, Mary, 148
Old age, 55, 74, 179
opportunity, xi, xiv, 25, 40, 42, 97, 132, 140, 172, 176, 231, 263
Organization Man, 4

P

P.G.A. tournaments, 74
Palmyra, 183, 184
Paradox of Riches, The, 142
parapsychology, 245, 248
pastors, 80
Patton, 138
Peale, Norman Vincent, 108, 192, 277
Penn, William, 118
persistence, 73, 74, 75, 146, 150, 234
philanthropist, 98, 135

Philippines, 99
Physical concerns, 63, 215
physical goals, 157, 158, 160, 199
physical reality, 90, 154
physiological transmittals, 116
Piper Super Cub, 49
Plato, 56, 245
political elites, 91
Pontius Pilate, 90
positive emotions, 63, 143, 153
poverty, 2, 5, 11, 15, 22, 46, 65, 80, 155, 190, 193, 212, 255, 256
power, 7, 9, 28, 34, 37, 44, 50, 51, 52, 60, 67, 70, 75, 76, 78, 86, 87, 90, 96, 97, 98, 100, 108, 109, 112, 117, 127, 129, 132, 133, 157, 158, 159, 160, 170, 171, 175, 193, 194, 195, 198, 210, 223, 232, 250
prayer, 39, 40, 44, 59, 85, 107, 108, 113, 222, 228, 245, 247, 249
prejudice, 96, 132, 231
President Ronald Reagan, 83
Presley, Elvis, 142
Procrastination, 131, 230
Psalm 15,
A Psalm of David, 105
Psalm 23, 51, 260
psychics, 244, 249
Puryear, Edgar 138
Pyramids, 34

Q

Quantico, VA, 3
Quantum Mechanics, 246

R

Reagan, Ronald, 108
Real estate, 48
Realtor, vii, 279, 280

RECOGNITION OF SELF-
   EXPRESSION, 90
redemption, 91
refugee camps, 81
religious extremism, 118
renaissance man, vii, 280
Republican party, 33
Retirees, 81
retirement, xv, xvii, 13, 45, 56, 87, 96, 143, 157, 164, 189, 224
Reuwer, Ken, ix
Revenge, 63, 64, 85, 216, 222
Reynolds, Debbie, 254
Rio Grande, 2
robber barons, 33
Robinson, Jackie 118
Rockefeller, 83, 142
Rockwell, Willard F., 79
Rocky Graziano, 30
romance, 3, 63, 64, 215
Rommel, 138
Roosevelt, F.D., 116
Rules, 196
Rush University, 76
Rose, Pete, 74, 75

Self Expression, 92, 226
Self-conceit, 38
Self confidence, 230, 234
self-control, 50, 51, 89, 108
self-hypnosis, 40, 41, 112, 133, 170
selfishness, 62, 131, 167, 231
Self-Preservation, 89, 92, 226
Senator Bernie Sanders, (see Sanders, Bernie)
Seven Basic Fears, 50, 51, 154, 197
Seven Negative Emotions, 63, 64, 216
sex, 63, 64, 89, 111, 151, 153, 215, 235, 265
Sexuality, 93, 227
Shakespeare, 9, 25, 35, 45, 61, 94, 97, 108, 134, 135, 142, 184, 193, 203, 228, 248
Sheen, Martin, 192
Shenandoah National Park, 17, 18
Shenandoah Valley, 249, 250, 255
Sherwood, Ben, 52
Shore, Dinah, 192
Shylock, 118
Silicon Valley, 142
Sinatra, Frank, 3
Slim, Carlos, 190
Snead, Sam, 74
Social involvements, 63, 215
Social Security, xvii
social workers, 1, 80
Society of Actuaries, 55
soul mates, 54
soul-like characteristics, 53
Soviet Union, 83
Spain, 182
Spark, Murial, 177
specific goals, 76, 101, 147
Spiritual needs, 63, 215
spirituality, 77, 131, 165, 220, 230
Spitefulness, 115
St. John, 183, 184
St. Paul, 56, 256

S

saddle bum, 6
Saint, 183, 200, 246
Saintly Solutions, 129
saint's mission, 66
Salvation Army, 1
Sanders, Bernie, 139
Sanders, Colonel Harlan, 190
Scholar, 183, 200
School of Love, 193
Script, i, 9, 10, 11, 12, 41, 98, 140, 197, 280
Scripture, 10
Schwab, Charles, 16
Seattle Longitudinal Study, 97
Secret of the Ages, The, 151
Secrets of Mind Power, The, 170

St. Vincent, 31
Statement of Exchange, 160
Statement of Goals, 70, 207, 218
Statement of Your Goals, 69, 198, 217
Strategic Counterintelligence Directorate (SCID, xv
Stevenson, Robert Louis 191
Stone, W. Clement 6, 98
Stowe, Harriet Beecher, 192
Stress, 81
subconscious, 9, 13, 40, 41, 42, 44, 50, 69, 84, 112, 133, 134, 148, 149, 153, 154, 155, 158, 160, 171, 192, 199
subconscious mind, 9, 13, 40, 41, 42, 84, 112, 133, 134, 148, 149, 153, 154, 155, 158, 171, 192, 199
Successful aging, 143, 148
suggestion, 154, 158, 159, 160, 170
suicide, 16, 62
superstition, 52, 63, 64, 85, 216, 222, 132, 231
Schweitzer, Albert, 108

T

telepathy, 9. 42, 244, 246, 248-250
Tennyson, 62
thought patterns, 9, 23, 24, 26, 31, 145, 197, 233, 247
Titus Oates', 183
Tolerance, 115, 145, 233
Treasure island, 191
triumph, 128
Trump, Donald. 31, 32, 33, 34, 35, 83, 116,
Truth and Justice, 43

U

U.S. Steel, 73
U.S.S. Cole, xi

Uncle Tom, 118, 192
UNITY, 81
Universal Mind, 157
University of Rochester, 151

V

valiant, 183
vanity, 62
Vindictive attitude, 132, 232
Virginia Tech, xiv
vision, 10, 13, 81, 100, 118, 177
visualizing, 153
vulgarity and slander, 132, 232

W

Wagner, Richard, 191
Wall Street, 16, 33
Wall Street wolf men, 33
Wal-Mart Stores, 99
Walton, Sam, 99
Wallace, Henry, 255
Walter Reed, 3
Washington, 3, 18, 103, 253, 279
Watts, 18
wealth, 1, 4, 6, 7, 11, 12, 16, 17, 25, 29, 32, 33, 34, 47, 48, 51, 68, 97, 108, 137, 141, 142, 191, 211, 252, 280
Whitney, Richard 16
Whittier, 123
Wickedness, 115, 258
Widemarsh Common, 183
Wikipedia, 198
Wilder, Laura Ingalls, 190
Wilson, Kemmons, 84
wisdom, 32, 58, 81, 86, 108, 139, 151, 166, 176, 191, 194, 195, 199, 204, 223, 280
wise men, 46, 78, 203
WORDS and FIRE, 10
work effort, 131, 231
World War II, 82, 99, 138, 178
wrongful thoughts, 207

BIBLIOGRAPHY (all available at Amazon.com)

THE RICHEST MAN IN BABYLON, George S. Clason, A Signet Book, 1988

SUCCESSFUL AGING, Mary O'Brien, M.D. BIOMED BOOKS, 2005

THE TYCOONS, Charles R. Morris, TIMES BOOKS, 2005

CONSCIOUSLY CREATING CIRCUNMSTANCES, George Winslow Plummer, Society of Rosicrucians, Inc. 1990

JUST AS I AM, Bill Graham, Guidepost, 1997

THE GREAT THOUGHTS, George Seldes, BALLANTINE BOOKS, 1985

CREATORS, Paul Johnson, HarperCollins, 2006

HOW I TURNED $50 INTO 5 MILLION IN COUNTRY PROPERTIES,

B.K. Haynes, Greatland Publishing Co., 2004

HOW YOU CAN GROW RICH THROUGH RURAL LAND, Starting from Scratch, B.K. Haynes, Greatland Publishing Co., 1979.

AS A MAN THINKETH, James Allen, Barnes & Noble, 1992

SELF HYPNOTISM, Leslie M. LeCron, A Signet Book, 1964

THE MAGIC OF BELIEVING, Claude M. Bristol, Amazon 1978

THINK LIKE A BILLIONAIRE, Donald J. Trump, Random House, 2004

TRUMP, Donald J. Trump, Surviving At The Top, Random House, 1990

THE ART OF THE DEAL, Donald J. Trump, Amazon

THE ART OF THE COMEBACK, Donald J. Trump, 1997, Times Books

THE VIRTUE OF PROSPERITY, Dinish D'souza, The Free Press, 2000

LIFE AFTER DEATH, Dinish D'souza, 2009

THINK AND GROW RICH, Napoleon Hill, Amazon

HOW TO WIN FRIENDS AND INFLUENCE PEOPLE, Carnegie, Amazon

THE SECRET OF THE AGES, Collier, Amazon

ACRES OF DIAMONDS, Conwell, Amazon

THE GOLDEN AGE, Collier, Amazon

EMERSON'S ESSAYS, Amazon

THE POWER OF WILL, Haddock, Amazon

YOU CAN WORK YOUR OWN MIRACLES, Napoleon Hill, Amazon

SUCCESS THROUGH A POSITIVE MENTAL ATTITUDE, Napoleon Hill, Amazon

GROW RICH WITH PEACE OF MIND, Napoleon Hill, Amazon

THE POWER OF POSITIVE THINKING, Norman Vincent Peale, Amazon

COMMON BIBLE, Collins

LAWS OF SUCCESS, Napoleon Hill, Amazon

HOW I TURNED $1,000 INTO 3 MILLION IN REAL ESTATE, Nickerson

ALL ABOUT GOALS AND HOW TO ACHIEVE THEM, Addington

SUCCESS, MOTIVATION, AND THE SCRIPTURES, Cook

SECRETS OF MIND POWER, Lorayne

THE GREATEST SALESMAN IN THE WORLD, Mandino

THE GREATEST SECRET IN THE WORLD, Mandino

THE SUCCESS SYSTEM THAT NEVER FAILS, Stone

NINETEEN STARS, Puryear, Amazon

GET ANYONE TO DO ANYTHING, David J. Lieberman, St Martin's Griffin, 2000

I DARE YOU, William Danforth, Amazon

THE 5 LESSONS A MILLIONAIRE TAUGHT ME, Evans, Simon & Schuster, 2006

THE SURVIVORS CLUB, Sherwood, Grand Central Publishing, 2009

THE idealESTATE MAN, Bradley K. Haynes, Greatland Publishing Co. 1978

POSITIVE THINKING FOR EVERY DAY OF THE YEAR, Norman Vincent Peale, 2000

LIFE REIMAGINED, Barbara Bradley Hagerty, Riverhead Books, 2016

THE TRUMPS, A Touchstone Book, Simon & Schuster, 2001

THE PURPOSE DRIVEN LIFE, Warren, Zondervan, 2002

DEALING WITH PEOPLE YOU CAN'T STAND, Kirschner & Brinkman, McGraw-Hill, Inc. Revised

PROPHET OF PURPOSE – The Life of Rick Warren, Jeffery L. Sheler, Doubleday, 2009

THE GREATEST MINDS AND IDEAS, Little, Simon & Schuster, 2002

THERE IS A RIVER: THE STORY OF EDGAR CAYCE, Sugrue, A.R.E. Press 1942

THE HABITUAL MILLIONAIRE, B.K. Haynes, Greatland Publishing & Music Co. 2006

TRANSCENDENTAL MEDITATION, Gordon R Lewis, G/L Publications, 1975

HERALD OF THE NEW AGE, Ruth Montgomery, Ballantine Books, 1986

HEAVEN AND THE AFTERLIFE, James L Garlow, Bethany House Publishers, 2009

UNTO THE HILLS, Bill Graham, HarperCollins Christian Publishers, July 2014

ABOUT THE AUTHOR

The ex trail boss, B.K. (Brad) HAYNES is back as a guide for your life's journey. After 50 years as a "rags to riches" land broker (Accredited ALC) and a *"People's Doctor of Dealing with Life"* (PDDL) "B.K." has sold and developed over 300 square miles of land over four heavily-populated states in the mid-Atlantic U.S., creating tens of thousands of rural home sites and granting about 15 miles of trail easements to the Potomac and Appalachian Trail Association to link the Virginia and WVA trail systems. He has been called "The Pied Piper of country real estate" by *The Washington Post Magazine* and has been informally labeled as The Donald Trump of country properties by others. His varied books include three novels, *The IdealESTATE MAN; The SADDLE BUM, WEST OF BABYLON,* and non-fiction: *THE HABITUAL MILLIONAIRE, HOW YOU CAN GROW RICH THROUGH RURAL LAND –Starting from Scratch; HOW I TURNED $50 INTO 5 MILLION IN COUNTRY PROPERTY—part time;* and *THE 100 GREATEST COUNTRY PROPERTY ADS* and the Success and Inspirational book, *RACING PAST THE END OF LIFE.* Mr. Haynes was the 1993 president of Virginia's Realtors Land Institute, 1993 Land Realtor of the Year, and 1995 Regional V.P., Regions III and IV for VA, WVA, MD, DE, DC, KY, TN, NC and SC.

As an entertainer, song writer, producer, publisher, and radio host for the show, *Valley of the Stars*, Haynes has recorded eight music albums with his company, Safari Records, and published the informative CD, *50 WAYS TO BUY COUNTRY PROPERTY WITH LITTLE OR NO MONEY DOWN*. He has also co-produced the Branson Missouri show, *No. #1 Hits of the 60's* and is now aggressively racing through his 80's, while offering valuable hard-earned wisdom to those approaching, or currently advancing into the realm of Good Old Age. In addition to his role as a land broker, developer, editor, scholar, aviator, instructor, and author of two screen plays, Haynes is an educator, lifetime member of the CEO CLUB OF NEW YORK and was named a Businessman of the Year 2005 by The Republican Party and is a Realtor Emeritus in Virginia.

The B.K. Haynes saga begins when he switched saddles from running trail rides in the Blue Ridge Mountains to mounting up for the wild recreational land boom of the 60's—making millions, surviving the great recession of the Obama years and leaping from a deep financial hole to an extraordinary comeback when others would be scheduling trips to nursing homes. Along his fifty-year trip from rags to riches he discovered two key words, SCRIPT and FLAME, expressions that open the gates to success and wealth in life. The ageless principles in this book apply to any span of life or gender, whether retaining the warm blood of youth to correcting acquired bad habits in Good Old Age. B.K. Haynes is a true *renaissance* man, revealing in this book his strategy in the coming generational war against the elderly and offering a dynamic manifesto for success, along with a manual of his tactics when dealing with adversity in life.

With this manifesto in hand, and committed to your memory, you will be armed with the most powerful written weapon now available for wise agers struggling with the looming emotional battles facing the Greatest Generation and followers in their path through life. When committed to memorizing and following the 16 rules in this manifesto, you will find yourself winning the two almost inevitable skirmishes facing elders as they mellow through the stealing hours of time to (1) gain financial security, societal unity and respect; and (2) to secure strengthened spiritual enlightenment in an evolving material world, where it should be written in stone for the ages that *OLD LIVES* must still matter to us all.

Visit: www.scriptandflame.com

www.bkhaynes.com

Facebook: https://www.facebook.com/bkhaynesbooks/